WALWORTH

HISTORY TOUR

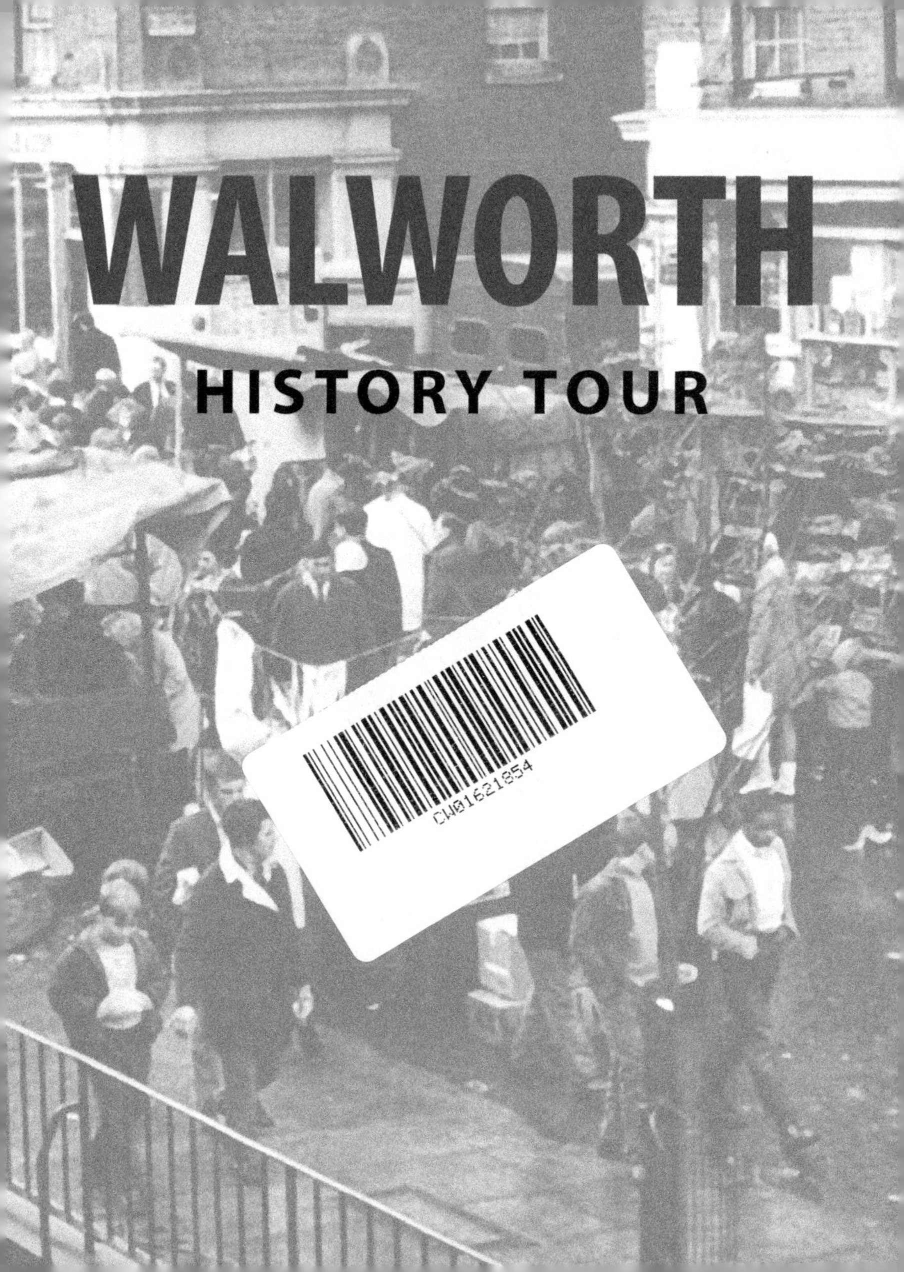

First published 2010
This edition published 2014

Amberley Publishing
The Hill, Stroud,
Gloucestershire, GL5 4EP
www.amberley-books.com

ISBN 978 1 4456 4152 2 (print)
ISBN 978 1 4456 4166 9 (ebook)

British Library Cataloguing in Publication Data.
A catalogue record for this book is available from the British Library.

Typesetting by Amberley Publishing.
Printed in Great Britain.

INTRODUCTION

The area of Walworth, London SE17, lies south of the River Thames and is a hustling, bustling area with a historic past. Its boundaries are the Elephant and Castle in the north, Kennington to the west, Camberwell to the south and the Old Kent Road in the east.

Looking at the area today, it's very hard to think of Walworth as anything other than an urban cityscape, lined as it is by the concrete blocks of the Heygate and Aylesbury housing estates, erected in the early 1970s on demolished and bomb-damaged wasteland. Shops of every sort line the main route through it, the Walworth Road: once a cart track that cut through the Walworth Common.

By looking into its past, we find the Romans knew of the location, as did the Anglo-Saxons. The latter named the area Wealawyrd or Waleorde, which translates into 'The Farm of the Britons' with Walworth, as it became, famous for its market gardens and orchards.

The area is mentioned in the Domesday Book of 1086, which describes the village life of the manor with corn growing in the fields and cows grazing on the meadowland.

It is said that a later inhabitant of the village was Sir William of Walworth, who became the Lord Mayor of London between 1373 and 1379. In 1381, Sir William mortally wounded Wat Tyler; the leader of the Peasants' Revolt of that year, as Tyler and his army marched into London. To mark this event a dagger was added to the coat of arms of the City of London.

In Walworth, among the usual high street shop names you'll find on the Walworth Road, you'll also find one or two older local establishments that have traded here for many years. Arment's Pie & Mash shop for example, established in 1914 and Baldwin's the herbalist health shop that began even earlier in 1844. There has also been a bespoke tailor at No. 187 for at least eighty years.

At the halfway point on the road, you'll find East Street Market, known locally as East Lane or simply 'The Lane'. The street market has been here officially since 1880, though trading occurred nearby in the surrounding streets for many years previously to that.

Notables associated with SE17 include silent film legend Charlie Chaplin, born over a shop on East Street in 1889, a fact commemorated by a plaque on a wall at the mouth of the market. Others include Maurice Micklewhite, better known to millions as film star Michael Caine, and Charles Babbage, considered by many as the originator of the modern computer.

Walworth has constantly changed over the decades: it never stands still and the influx of people from around the world who have settled in the area continues a trend started in 1840 with the arrival of the Irish immigrants escaping the potato famine of that year. Before long, the majority of 'well-to-do' residents were moving out and ten families were moving into houses built for one, resulting in severe over-crowding and slum conditions.

In the 1920s and 1930s, a quarter of all housing in Walworth was considered unfit for human habitation, and the demolition of these properties, coupled with the Second World War bomb damage caused to that still standing, left town planners with a clean slate when it came to the building of new homes.

Their answer to this problem was the construction of enormous council estates, namely the Heygate and the Aylesbury.

Now, not fifty years after they were built, the entire Heygate Estate buildings are due for demolition as part of a major regeneration programme planned for the Elephant and Castle end of Walworth, with 6,000 new homes planned. With substantial renovation also planned for the Aylesbury estate, once again this area is undergoing massive change.

So begins another chapter for this famous district of London.

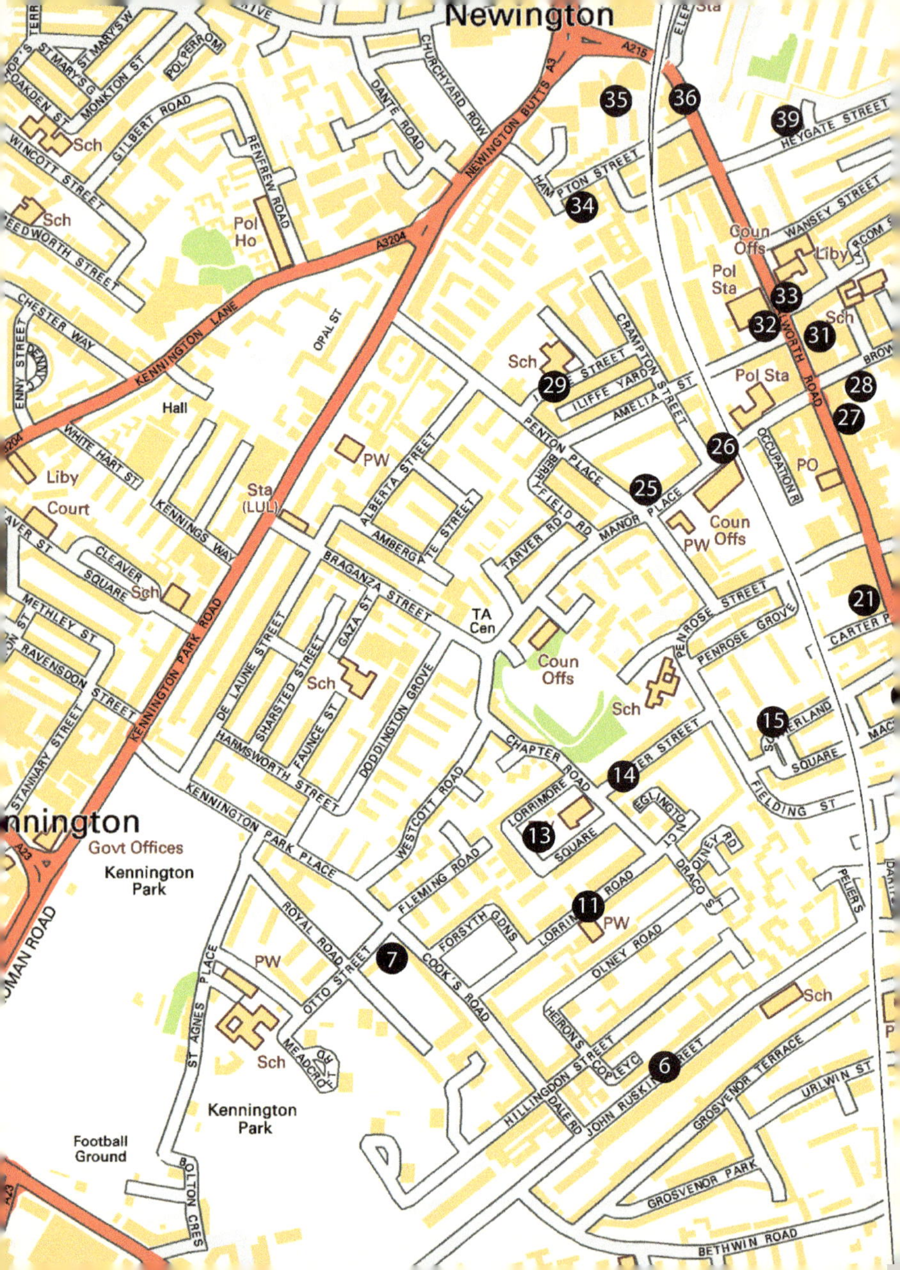

Newington
Kennington
Kennington Park
Football Ground
Govt Offices
NEWINGTON BUTTS
KENNINGTON LANE
KENNINGTON PARK ROAD
KENNINGTON PARK PLACE
HEYGATE STREET
WANSEY STREET
PENTON PLACE
MANOR PLACE
CHAPTER ROAD
JOHN RUSKIN STREET
GROSVENOR TERRACE
GROSVENOR PARK
BETHWIN ROAD
COOK'S ROAD
OLNEY ROAD
HARMSWORTH STREET
DE LAUNE STREET
BRAGANZA STREET
DODDINGTON GROVE
WESTCOTT ROAD
FLEMING ROAD
ROYAL ROAD
OTTO STREET
ST AGNES PLACE
BOLTON CRES
KENNINGS WAY
WHITE HART ST
CLEAVER SQUARE
METHLEY ST
RAVENSDON STREET
STANNARY STREET
GILBERT ROAD
RENFREW ROAD
WINCOTT STREET
CHESTER WAY
CHURCHYARD ROW
DANTE ROAD
ALBERTA STREET
AMBERGATE STREET
CRAMPTON STREET
ILIFFE YARD
AMELIA ST
PENROSE STREET
PENROSE GROVE
FIELDING ST
LORRIMORE SQUARE
LORRIMORE ROAD
HILLINGDON STREET
URLWIN ST
Sch
Pol Ho
Hall
Liby
Court
Sta (LUL)
PW
TA Cen
Coun Offs
Pol Sta
PO
35 36 39 34 33 32 31 29 28 27 26 25 21 15 14 13 11 7 6

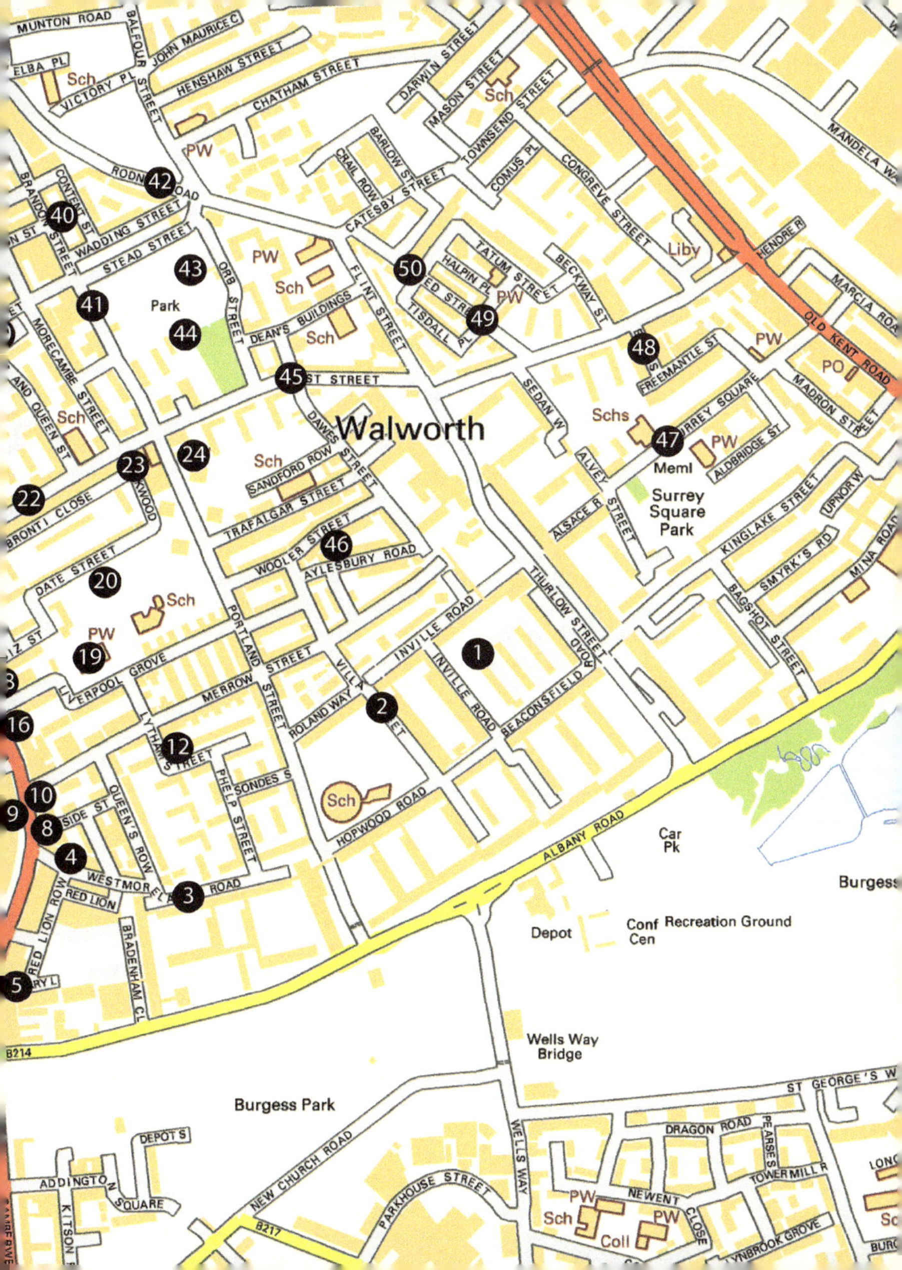

Walworth
MUNTON ROAD
BALFOUR STREET
JOHN MAURICE C
ELBA PL
VICTORY PL
HENSHAW STREET
CHATHAM STREET
DARWIN STREET
MASON STREET
TOWNSEND STREET
MANDELA WA
BARLOW ST
CRAIL ROW
CATESBY STREET
COMUS PL
CONGREVE STREET
RODNEY ROAD
BRANDON STREET
CONTENT ST
WADDING STREET
STEAD STREET
ORB STREET
Park
DEAN'S BUILDINGS
FLINT STREET
TATUM STREET
HALPIN PL
TISDALL PL
BECKWAY ST
HENDRE R
MARCIA ROA
OLD KENT ROAD
FREEMANTLE ST
MADRON STREET
PO
Liby
MORECAMBE STREET
AND QUEEN ST
EAST STREET
DAWES STREET
SEDAN W
SURREY SQUARE
ALDBRIDGE ST
Meml
Surrey Square Park
SANDFORD ROW
TRAFALGAR STREET
BRONTI CLOSE
ALVEY STREET
ALSACE R
KINGLAKE STREET
UPNOR W
WOOLER STREET
AYLESBURY ROAD
DATE STREET
THURLOW STREET
SMYRK'S RD
MINA ROAD
BAGSHOT STREET
PORTLAND STREET
INVILLE ROAD
VILLA STREET
BEACONSFIELD ROAD
LIVERPOOL GROVE
MERROW STREET
ROLAND WAY
LYTHAM STREET
PHELP STREET
SONDES S
SIDE ST
QUEEN'S ROW
HOPWOOD ROAD
ALBANY ROAD
WESTMORELAND ROAD
RED LION ROW
RED LION
BRADENHAM CL
Car Pk
Burgess
Depot
Conf Cen
Recreation Ground
Wells Way Bridge
B214
Burgess Park
ST GEORGE'S W
DRAGON ROAD
PEARSE S
TOWER MILL R
DEPOT S
ADDINGTON SQUARE
NEW CHURCH ROAD
PARKHOUSE STREET
WELLS WAY
NEWENT CLOSE
KITSON
B217
Coll
LYNBROOK GROVE
Sch
Schs
PW
1
2
3
4
5
8
9
10
12
16
19
20
22
23
24
40
41
42
43
44
45
46
47
48
49
50

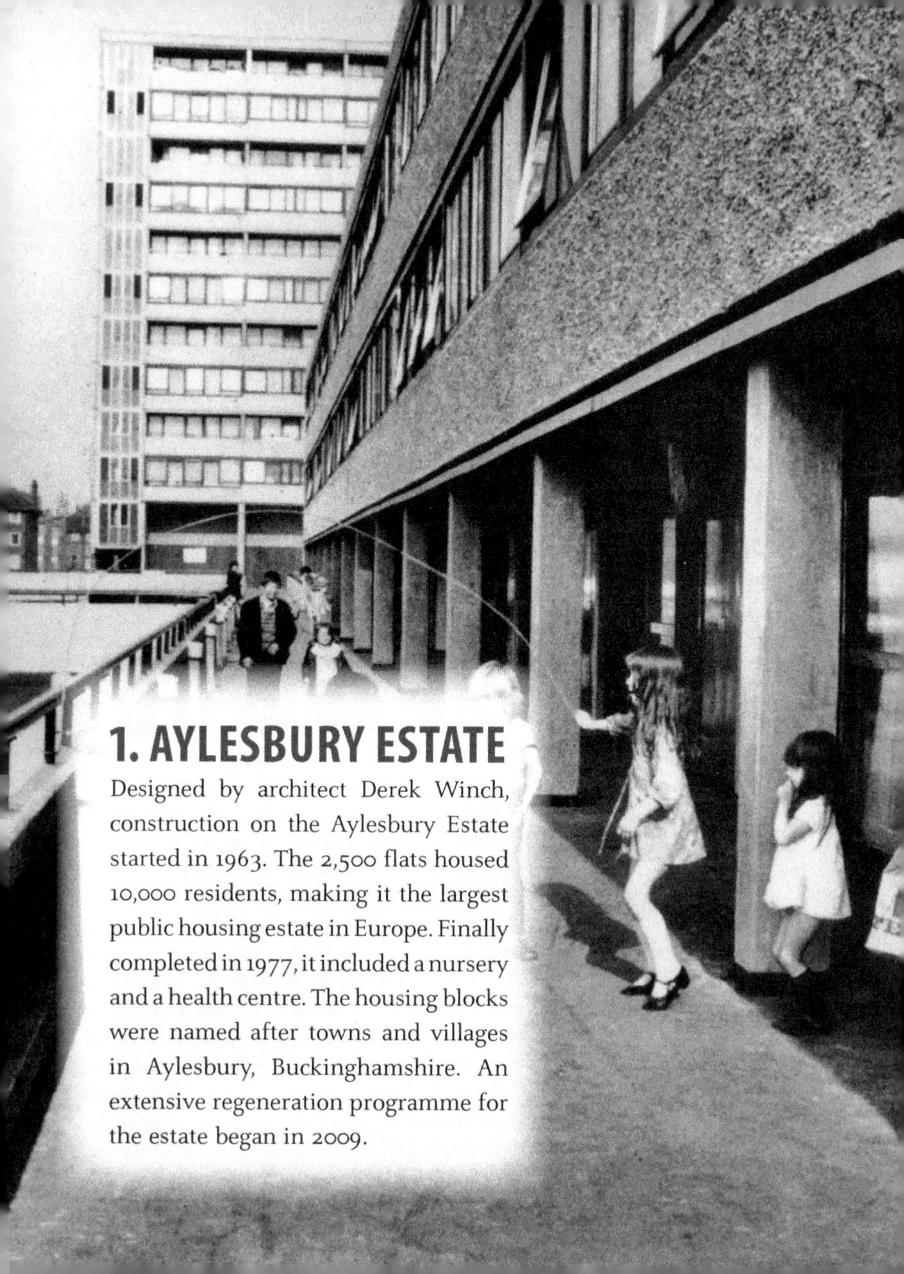

1. AYLESBURY ESTATE

Designed by architect Derek Winch, construction on the Aylesbury Estate started in 1963. The 2,500 flats housed 10,000 residents, making it the largest public housing estate in Europe. Finally completed in 1977, it included a nursery and a health centre. The housing blocks were named after towns and villages in Aylesbury, Buckinghamshire. An extensive regeneration programme for the estate began in 2009.

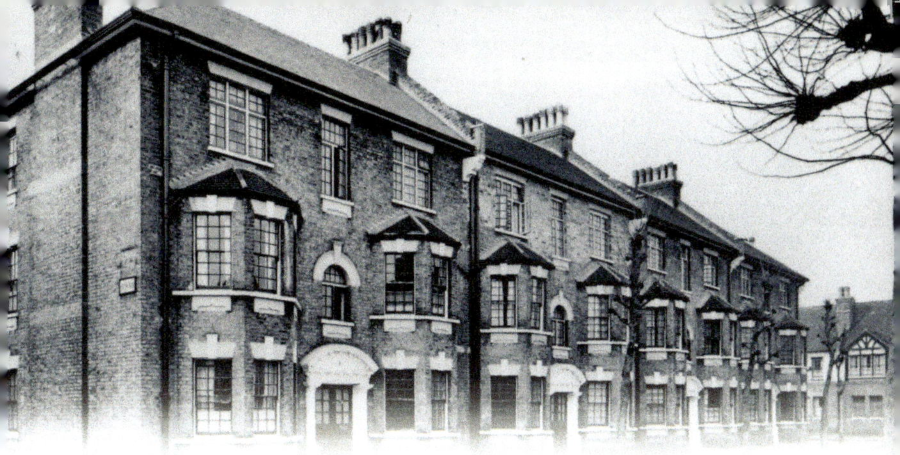

2. VILLA STREET

This street is part of the Octavia Hill Conservation Area. It is roughly 22 acres in size, and since 2006 has been owned and run by Grainger GenInvest. It was developed from slum housing in the early 1900s in conjunction with Hill, a social reformer and pioneer for affordable housing, with a special interest in city inhabitants, who later co-founded The National Trust. One former famous resident was long time Benny Hill sidekick, Jackie Mann. This conservation area provides 600 dwellings and there is a health centre at No. 47 Villa Street.

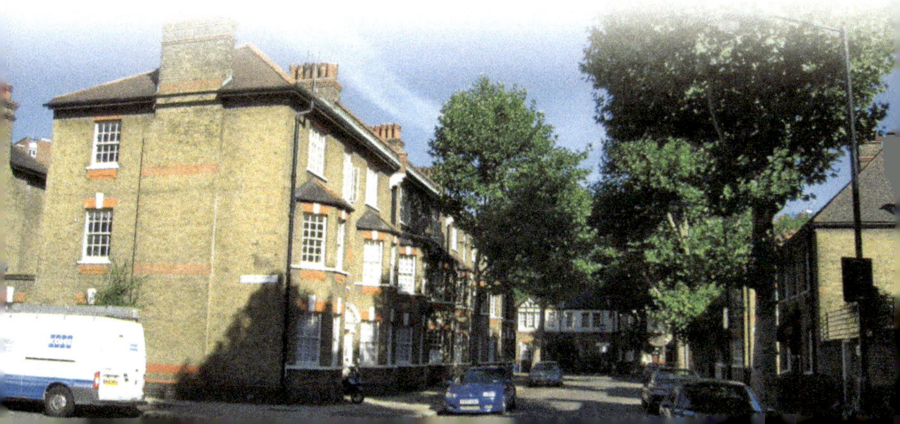

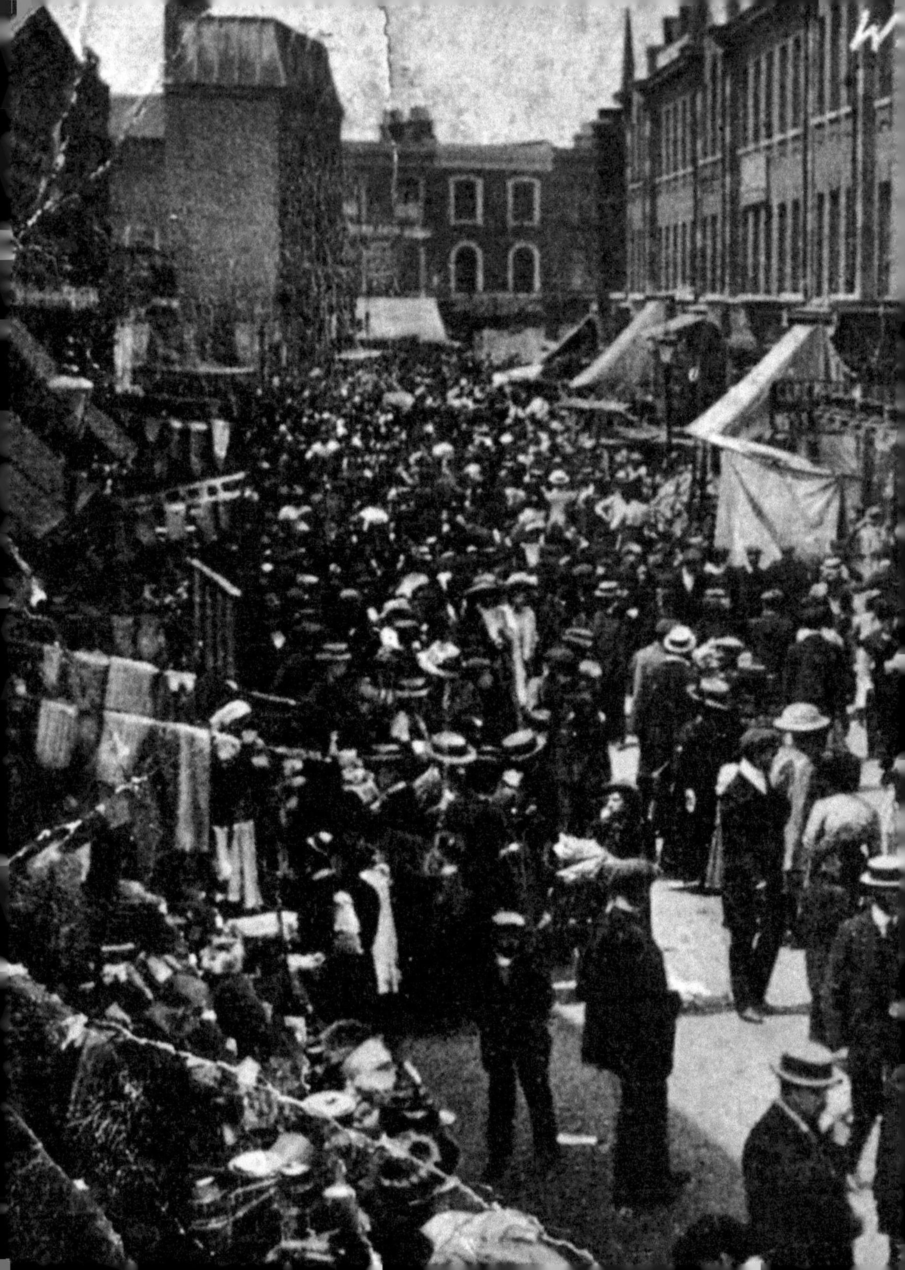

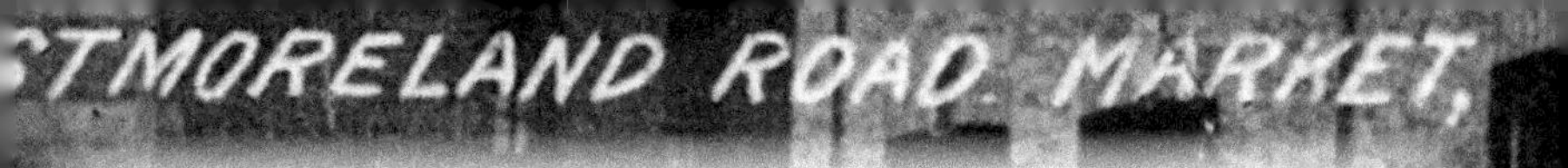

3. WESTMORELAND ROAD

For over 100 years there has been a market in this otherwise quiet side road. It drew 'totters' (better known as rag and bone men) from all over London to sell the old clothes they had collected. This tradition continues on Sunday mornings. Alongside the clothing stalls, a variety of electrical goods and a jumble of bric-à-brac can be also purchased. Once part of Walworth Common, it was also home to The Newington Institute Workhouse for the poor and destitute, which was built in 1885 and which housed up to a 1,000 people when it first opened. Described as a tall, grim building, it was demolished in 1969. Among its residents for a short while, were a young Charlie Chaplin and his brother Sydney. The Arment's Pie & Eel shop is situated at Nos 7–9.

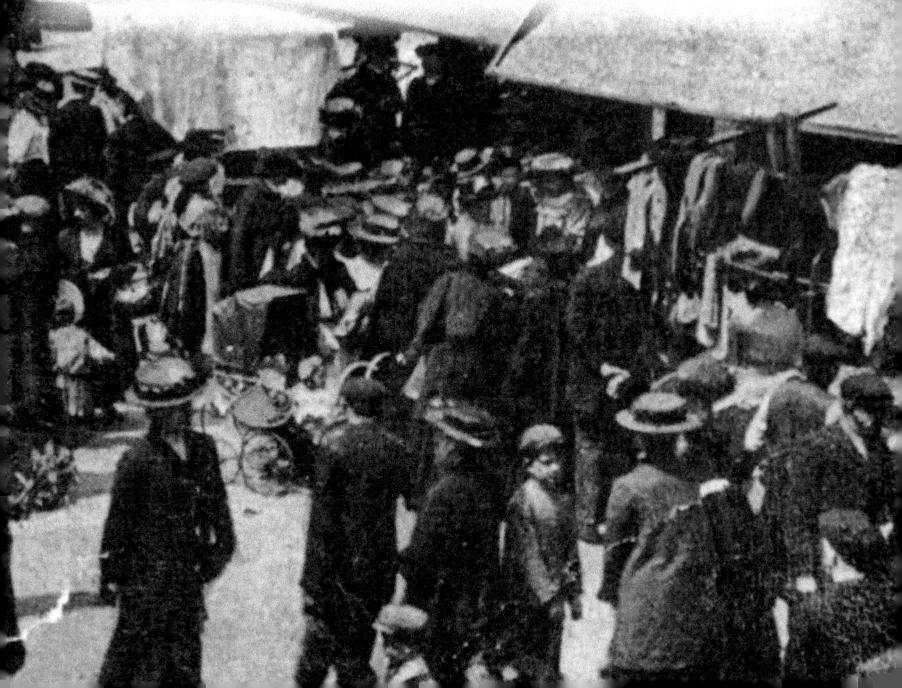

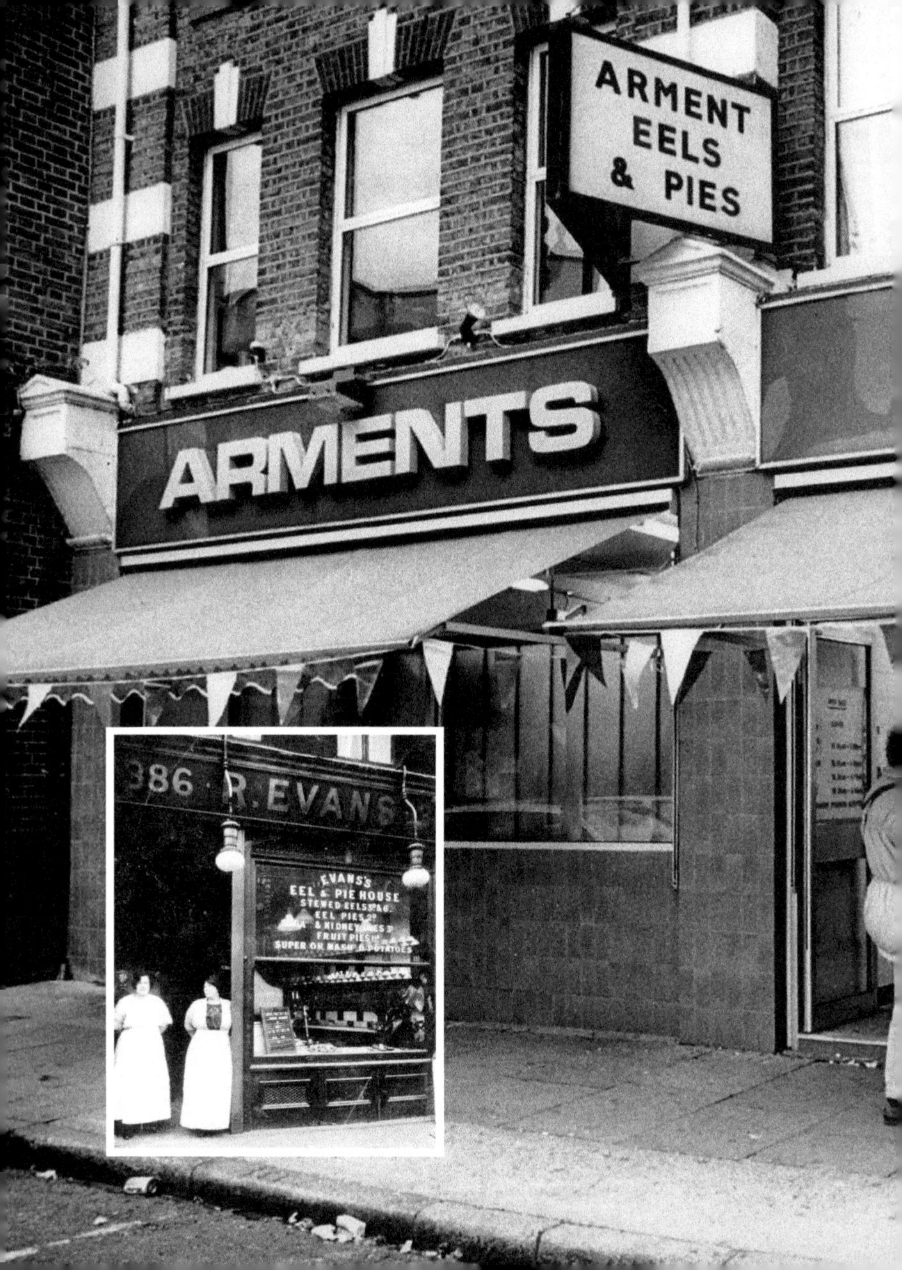
ARMENT
EELS
& PIES
ARMENTS
EVANS'S
EEL & PIE HOUSE

4. EVANS' EEL & PIE HOUSE

Arment's Pie & Mash is famous throughout the area of Walworth for its handmade steak pies, which are still made from a secret recipe. The Arment family bought the business from the Evans family in 1914, the old premises being at No. 386 Walworth Road. Emily (*right of inset*) was married to William Arment, and after taking the reins the shop was renamed. It moved to its current location, No 7–9 Westmoreland Road, in 1979. Arment's is still family run, with grandson Roy and his wife Cheryl now running the business.

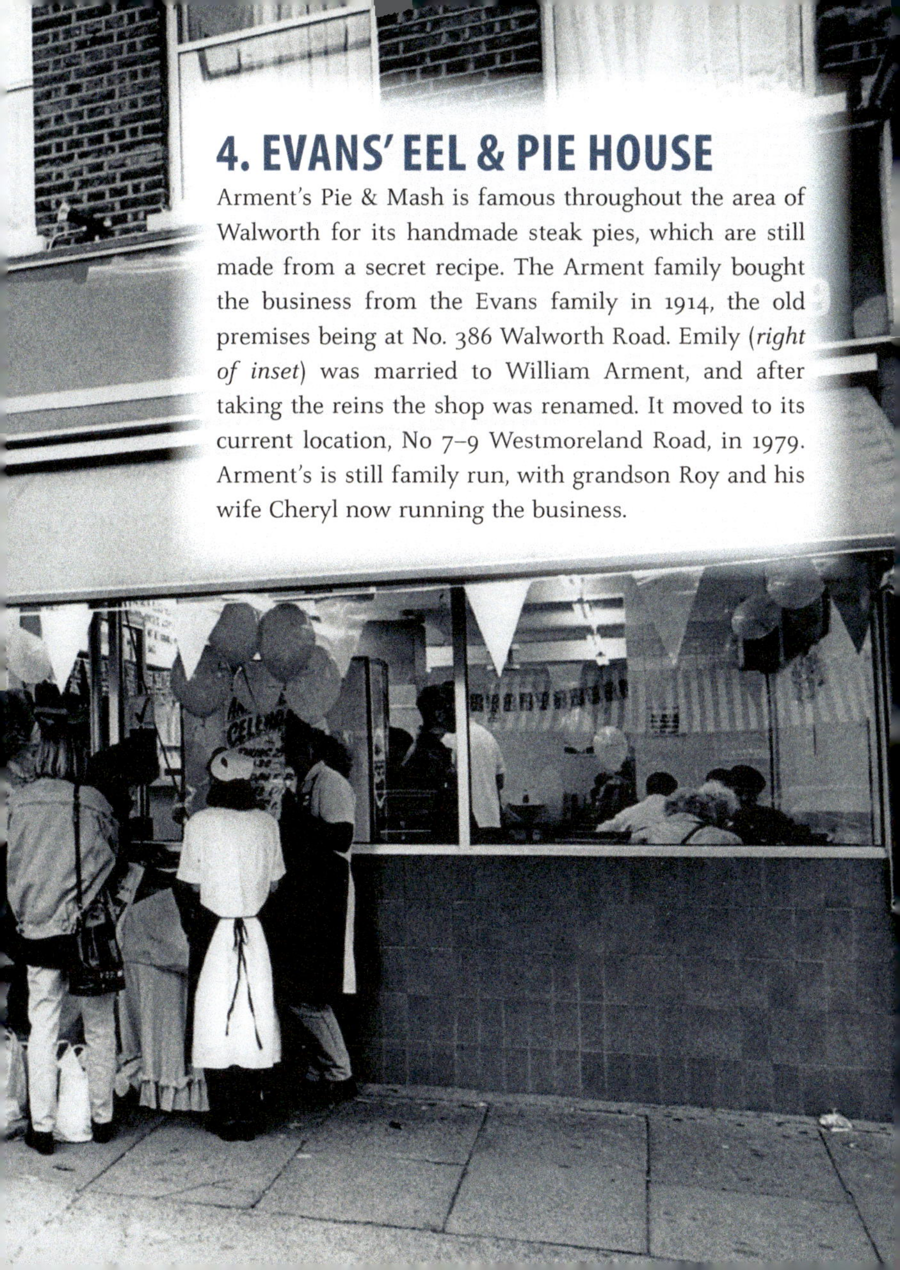

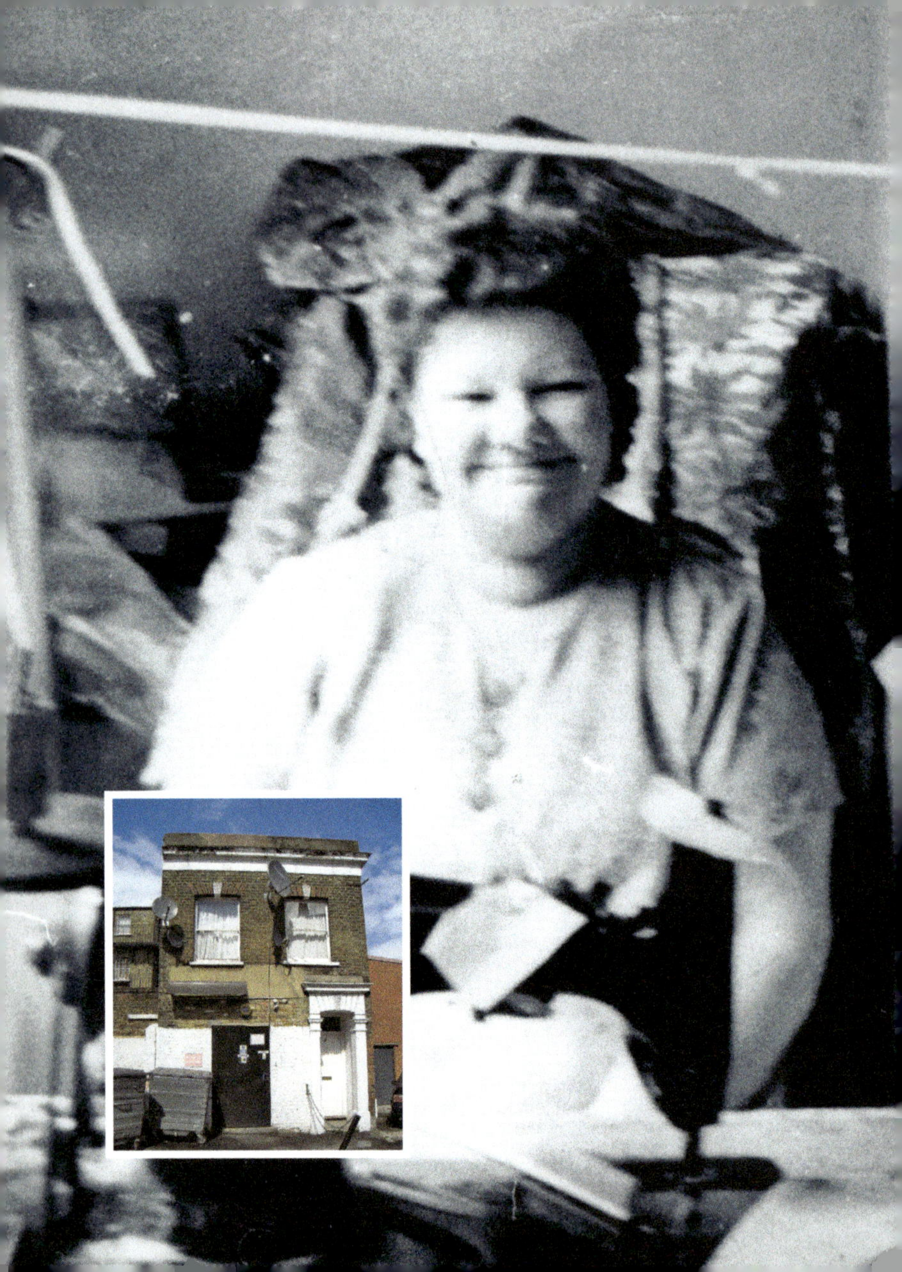

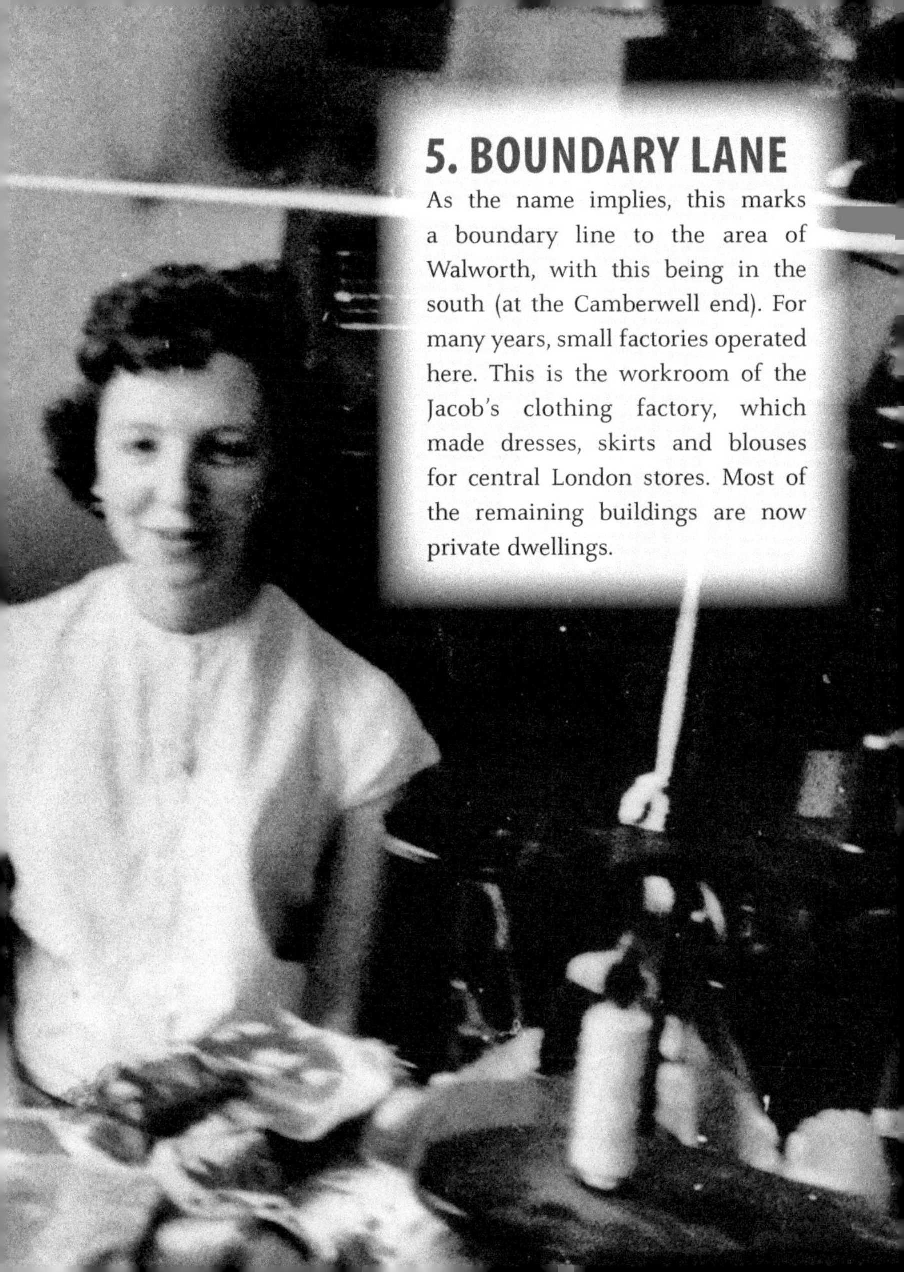

5. BOUNDARY LANE

As the name implies, this marks a boundary line to the area of Walworth, with this being in the south (at the Camberwell end). For many years, small factories operated here. This is the workroom of the Jacob's clothing factory, which made dresses, skirts and blouses for central London stores. Most of the remaining buildings are now private dwellings.

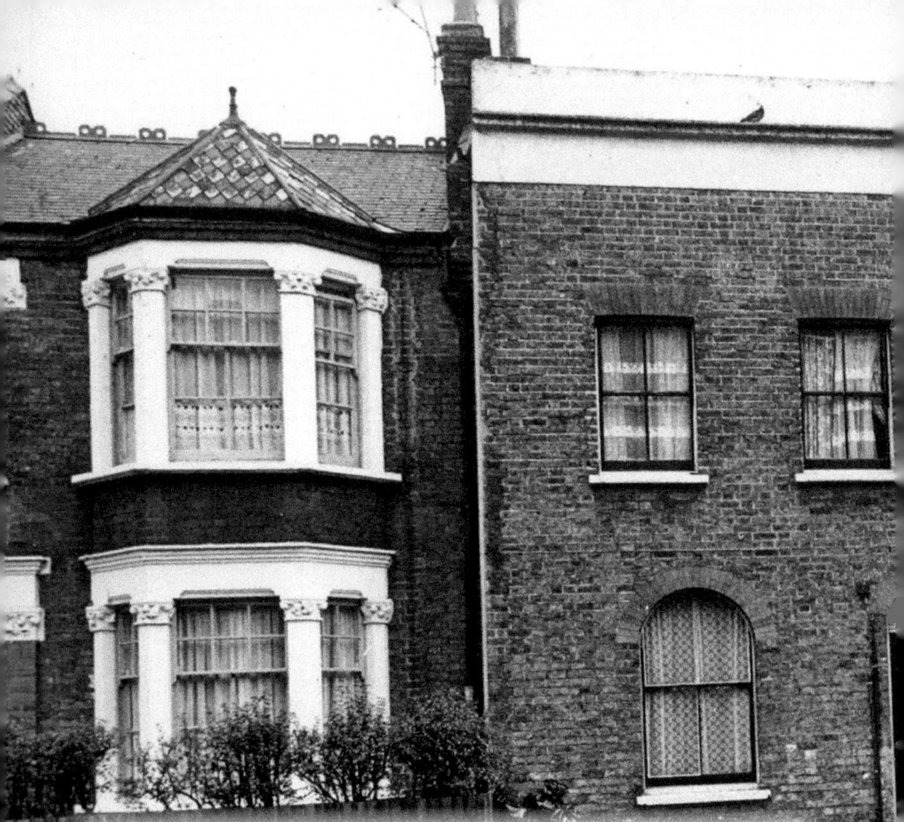

6. WHITBREAD MOSAIC

This fine example of mosaic work is found on a wall approximately halfway down John Ruskin Street on the South Side. It was formerly the rear entrance to the Grosvenor Tavern, the front being on Grosvenor Terrace, SE5. Both back and front are now houses. John Ruskin Street is so long that it begins in the SE5 postcode at its Walworth Road end and becomes SE17 in the middle, before returning to SE5 at the Camberwell New Road end.

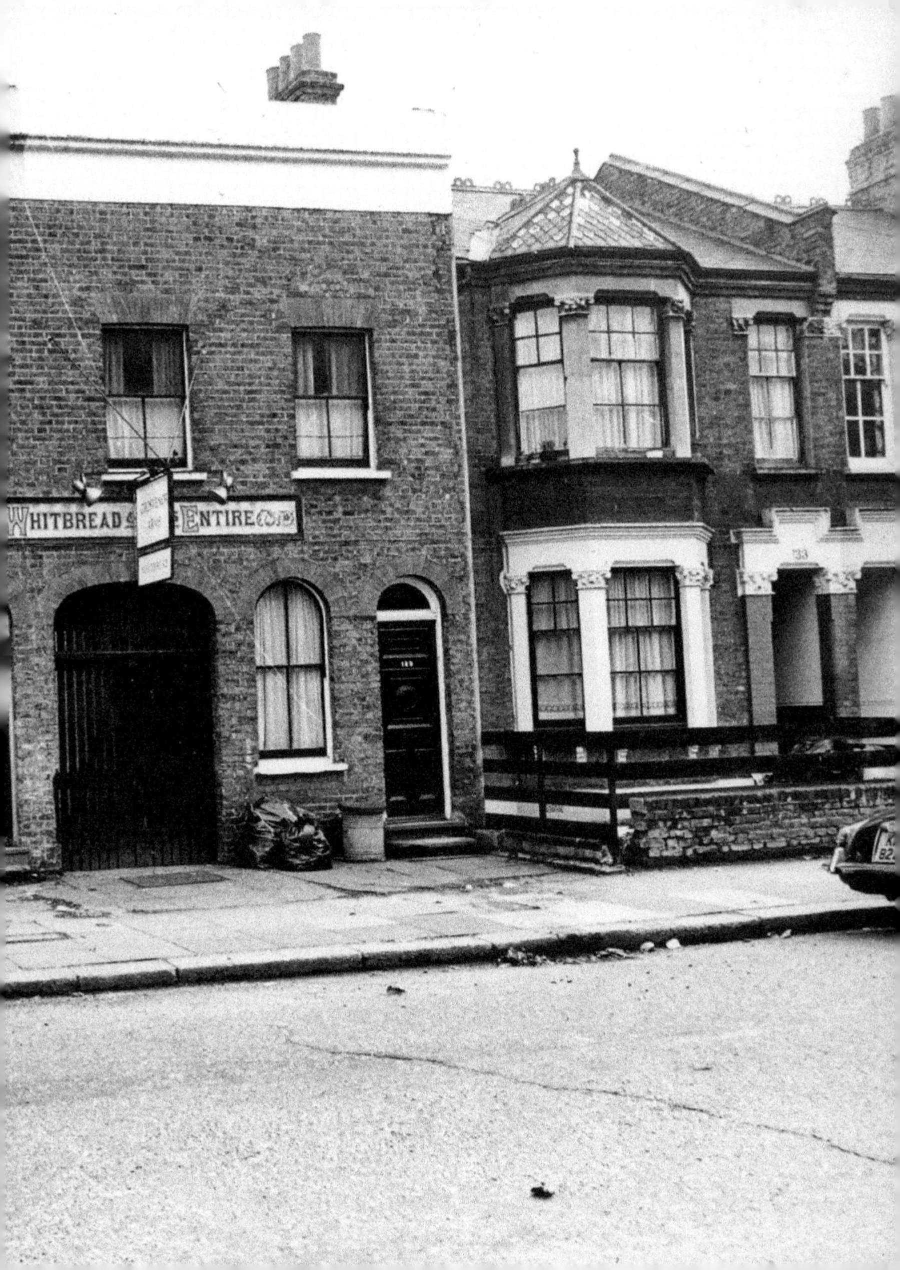
WHITBREAD
ENTIRE

7. THE BRANDON ESTATE

Named after Thomas Brandon, a late eighteenth-century land developer, this was one of the first high-rise developments in London. It contains six eighteen-storey and five twenty-five-storey blocks, a public library, a shopping precinct and a doctors' surgery. The tusk of a prehistoric mammoth was discovered when excavating began and is now displayed at the Cuming Museum.

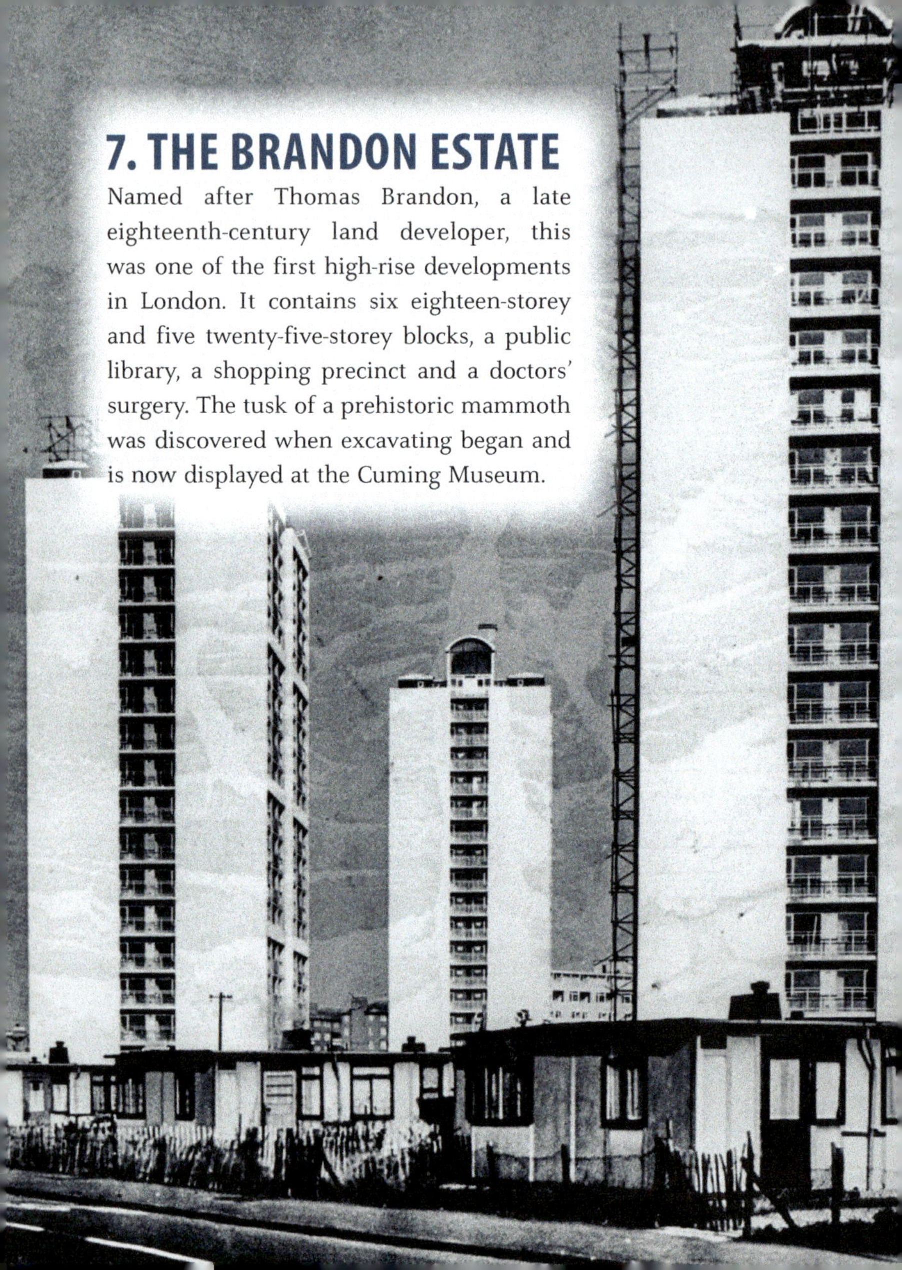

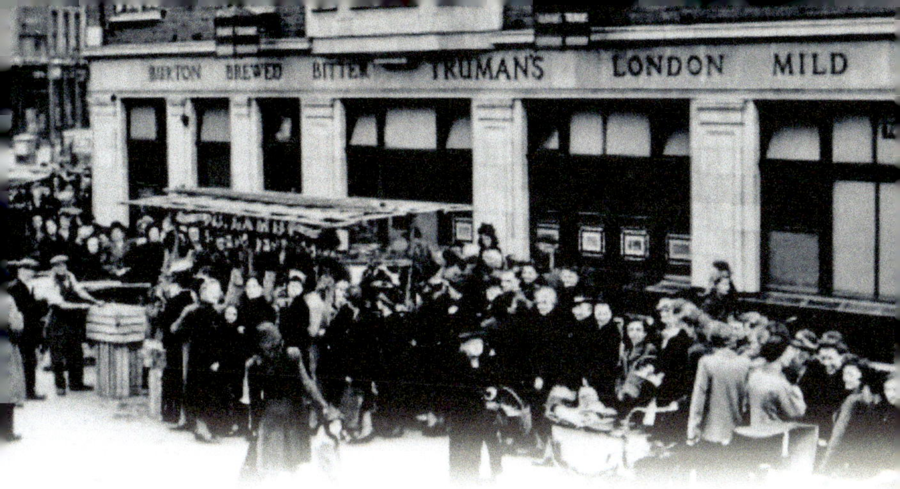

8. THE RED LION

Situated at No. 407 Walworth Road on the corner of Westmoreland Road, this pub is home to a mainly local Irish clientele. A Red Lion pub has stood here for over 200 years, with Red Lion Row nearby and Red Lion Mews once on the local map. The photograph above shows the queue for food rations in Westmoreland Road and clearly shows the exterior of the pub, which has changed little over the years. Hollywood film legend Clint Eastwood was recently seen in The Red Lion while filming his latest production *Hereafter*.

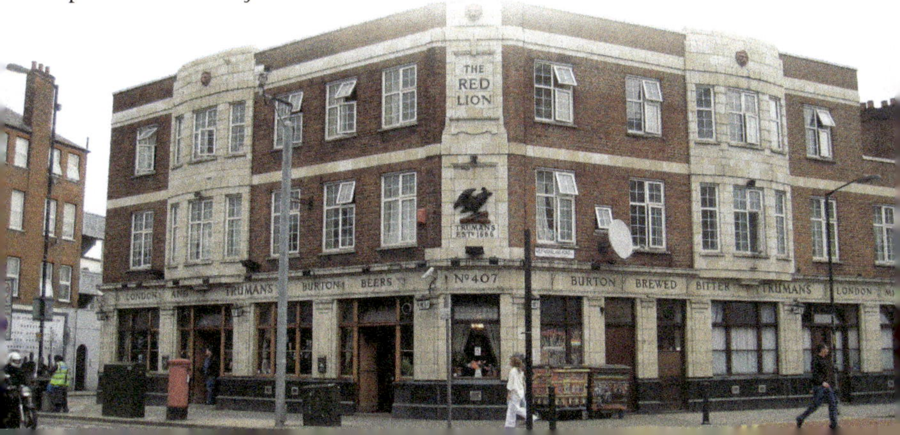

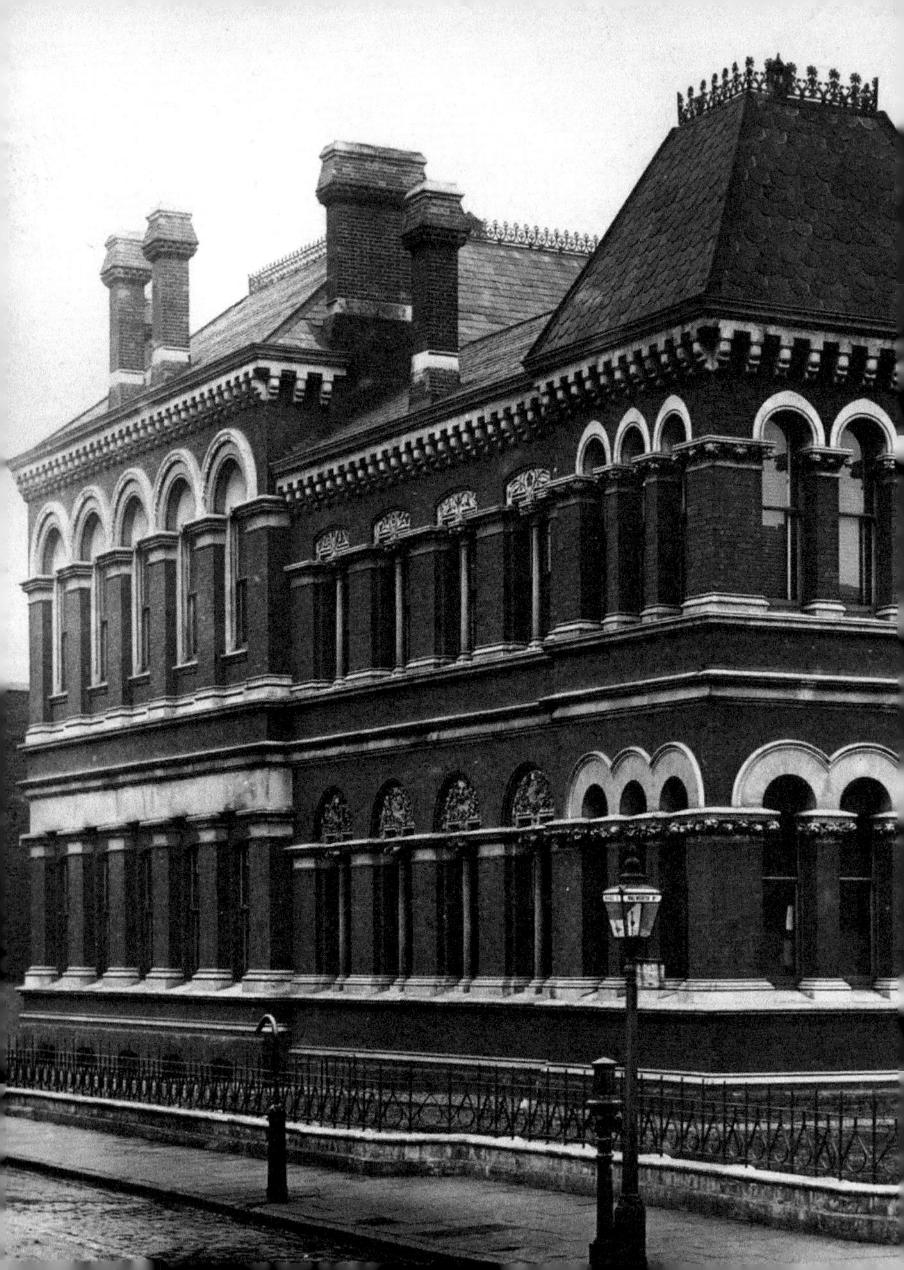

9. VESTRY HALL

The Grade II listed Vestry Hall incorporates Cuming Museum and Newington Public Library. Situated at No. 157 Walworth Road, the Vestry Hall of St Mary Newington was built in 1864 and was the seat of municipal authority, later to become the Town Hall for the Borough of Southwark between 1900 to 1965. It also later housed a registry office. An extension was added in 1900. Newington Public Library was constructed between 1892 and 1893 by builder J. Grover & Sons. The Cuming Museum, a gift to the borough by Henry Syer Cuming in memory of his father Richard, was built between 1902 to 1906. Acknowledged as one of London's finest local museums, it began with Richard Cuming collecting objects from the age of five.

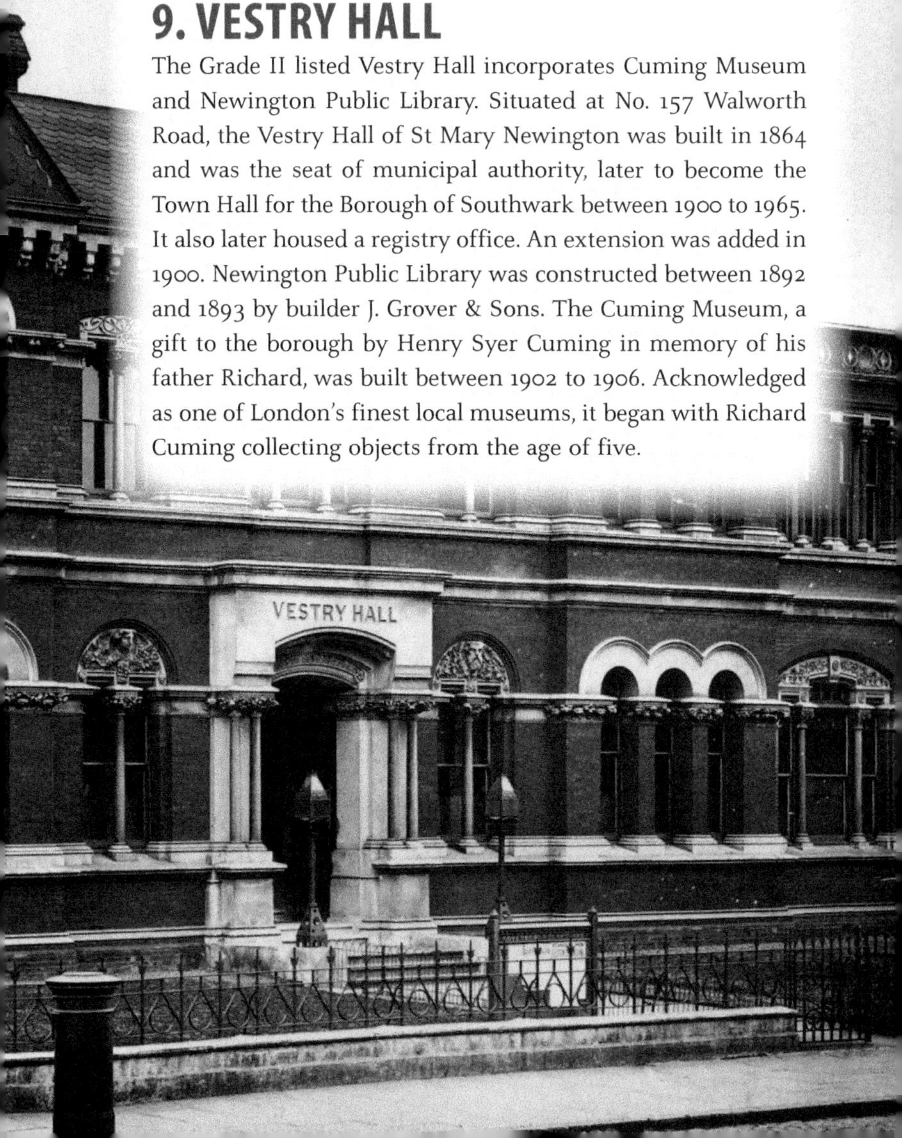

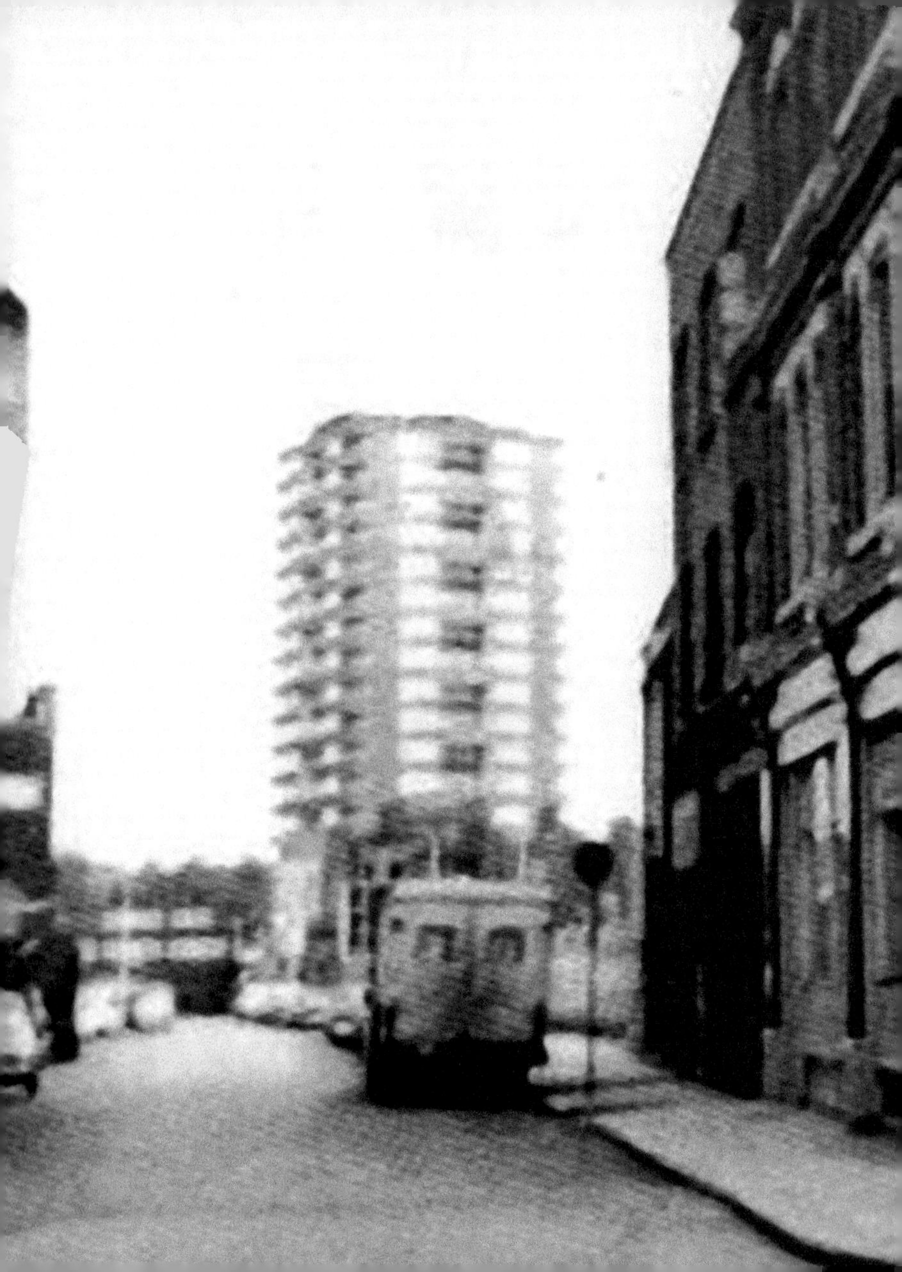

10. NO. 77 WALWORTH ROAD

The original Baldwin's herbalist shop began trading here in 1844. Forced to move in 1969 by development work on the Heygate Estate, the company relocated to its present address at No. 173 Walworth Road, later purchasing No. 171 in 1978. The area is now Elephant Road Park. In the background are the eighteen floors of Albert Barnes House, erected on New Kent Road in 1964.

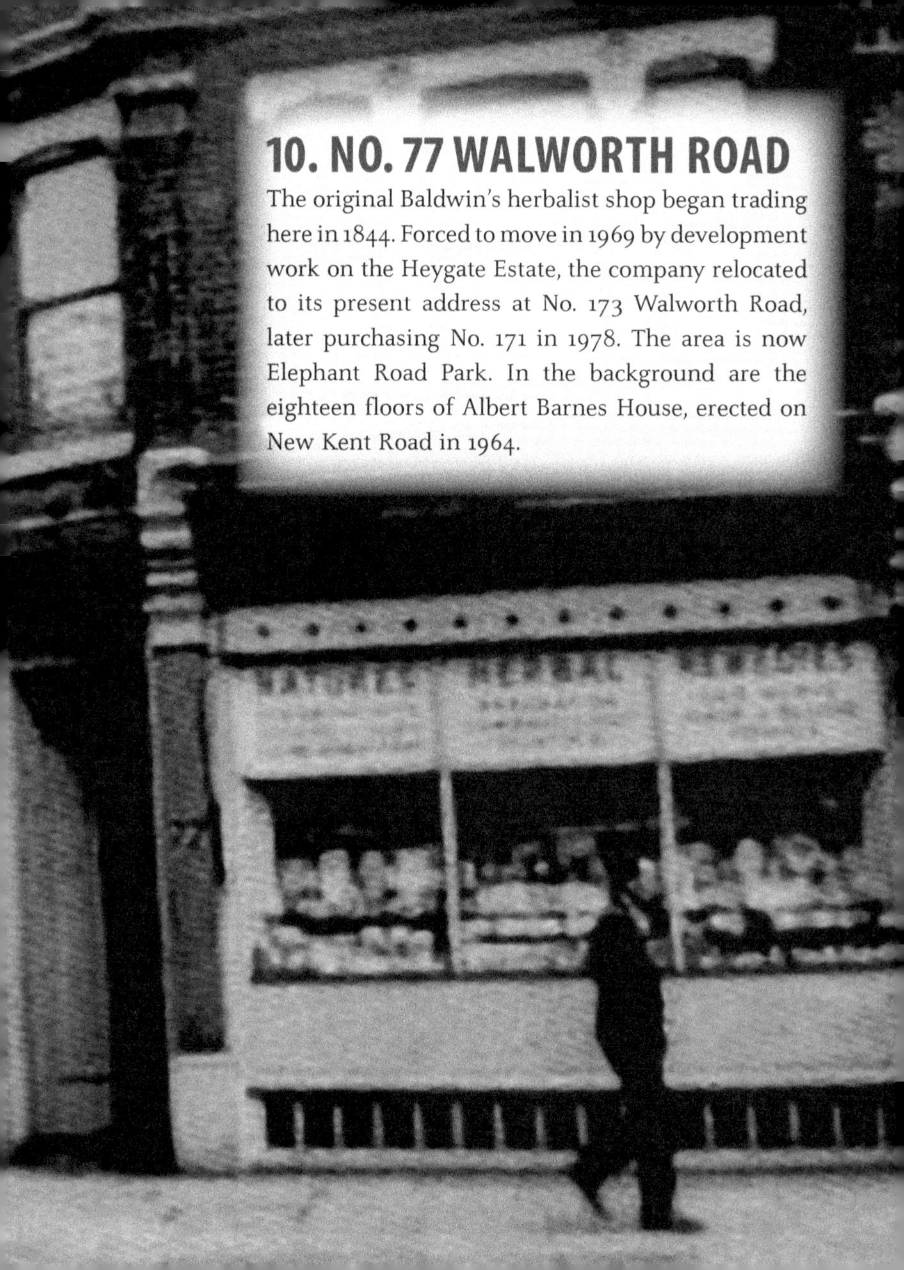

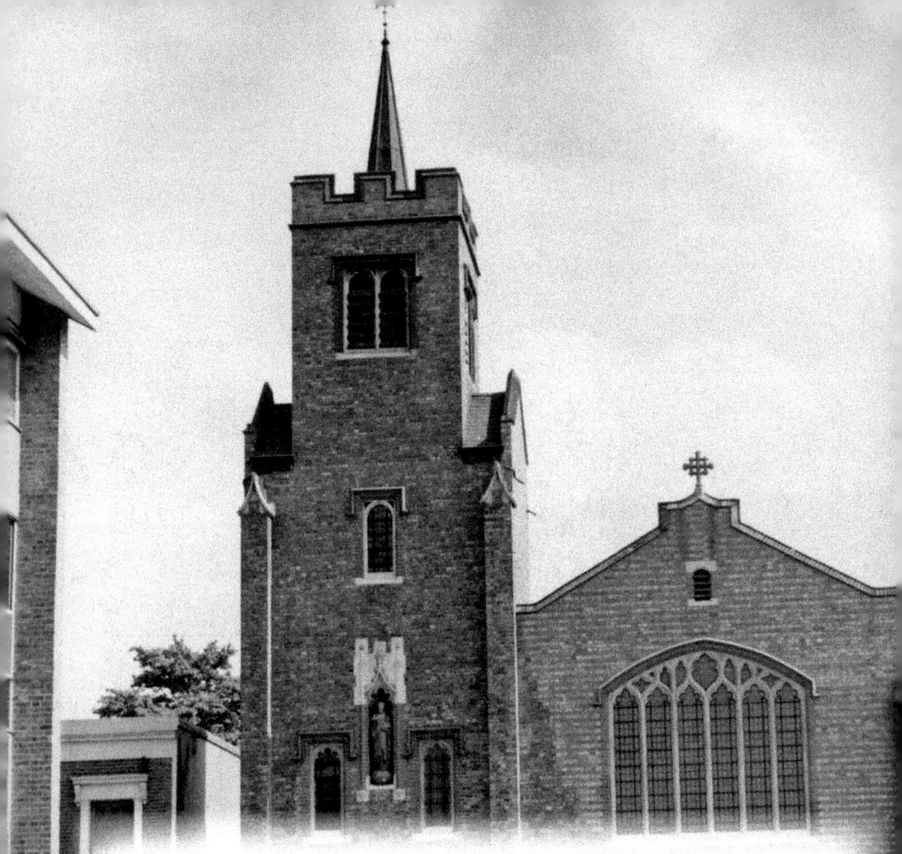

11. ST WILFREDS

Situated at No. 97 Lorrimore Road, this imposing structure was designed by Frederick Arthur Walters (1849–1931), a Scottish architect noted for his work on over fifty Roman Catholic churches. The clergy house at the English Martyrs church on Rodney Road is also the work of Walters. St Wilfreds was built in 1914 in 'perpendicular gothic' style in red brick, with a 60-foot tower topped by a small spire. It was bomb damaged in November 1940, and restored between 1948 and 1949.

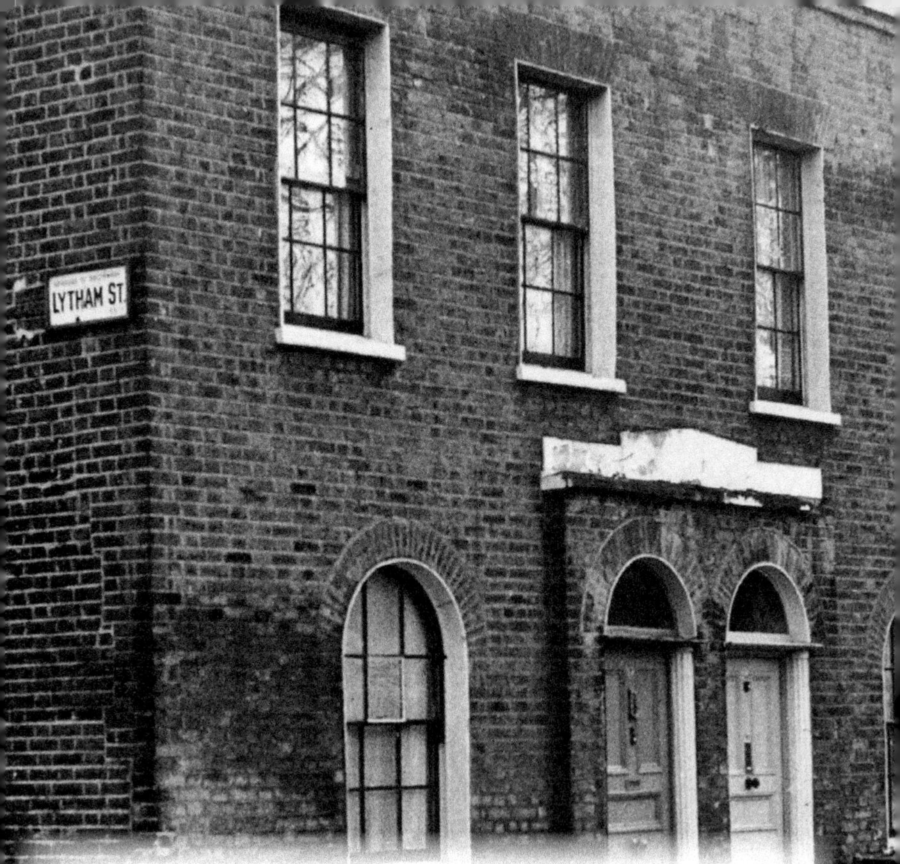

12. LYTHAM STREET

This fine Georgian house in the quiet back street of Liverpool Grove on the corner of Lytham Street has a stone plaque embedded in its side wall, which reads 'One Foot East Of This Wall Is The Property Of Mr Thomas Peacock'. The houses on Liverpool Grove are facing the south side of St Peter's church. Many have been restored to their former glory and are now very desirable residences in the area.

13. LORRIMORE SQUARE/ROAD

A map of Walworth from 1681 shows a common called 'Lattamore' or Lower Moor; 19 acres in size, that today is the location of Lorrimore Square. In 1769, Henry Penton leased the land from the ancient Dean and Chapter Estate. Records show it was grazing land up until 1831. House building began in the area around 1856. Today the houses on the eastern side of the square fall within the Sutherland Square Conservation Area.

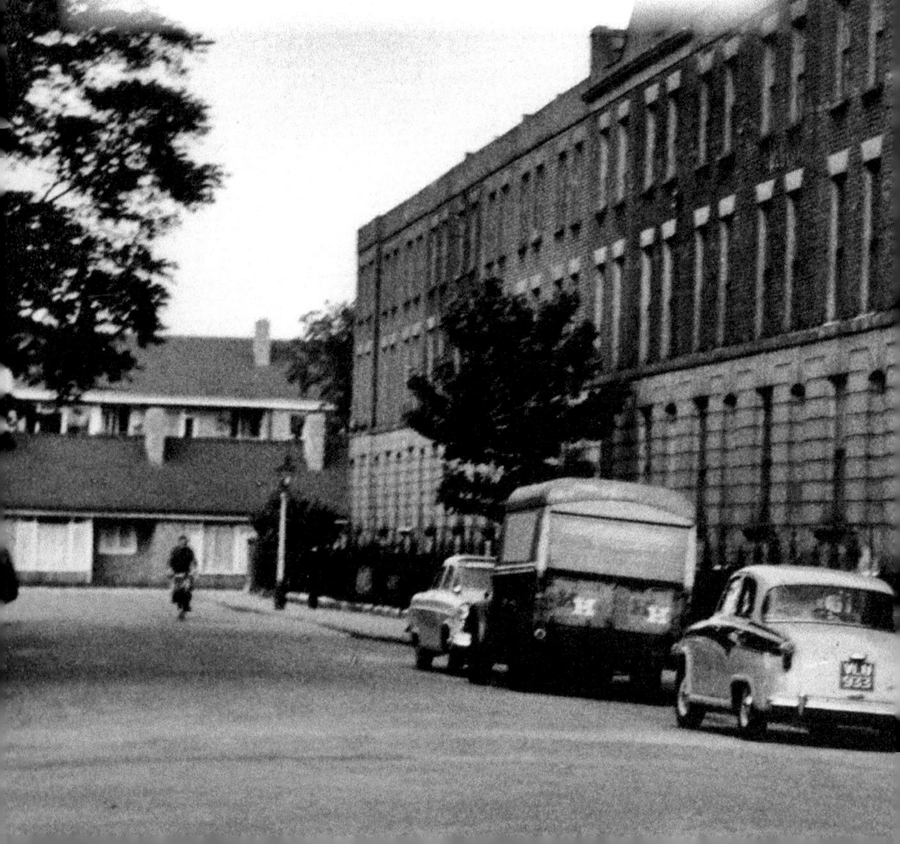

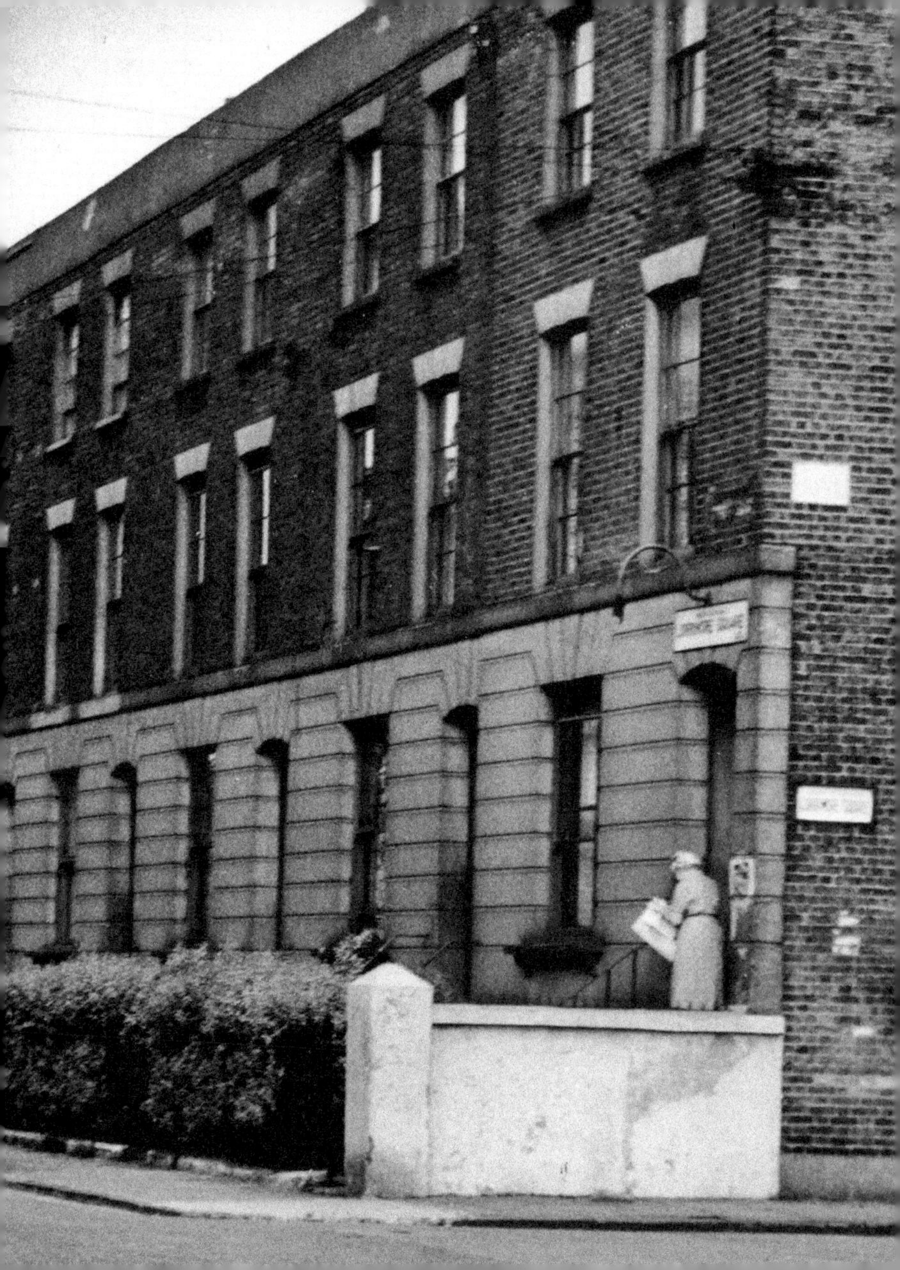

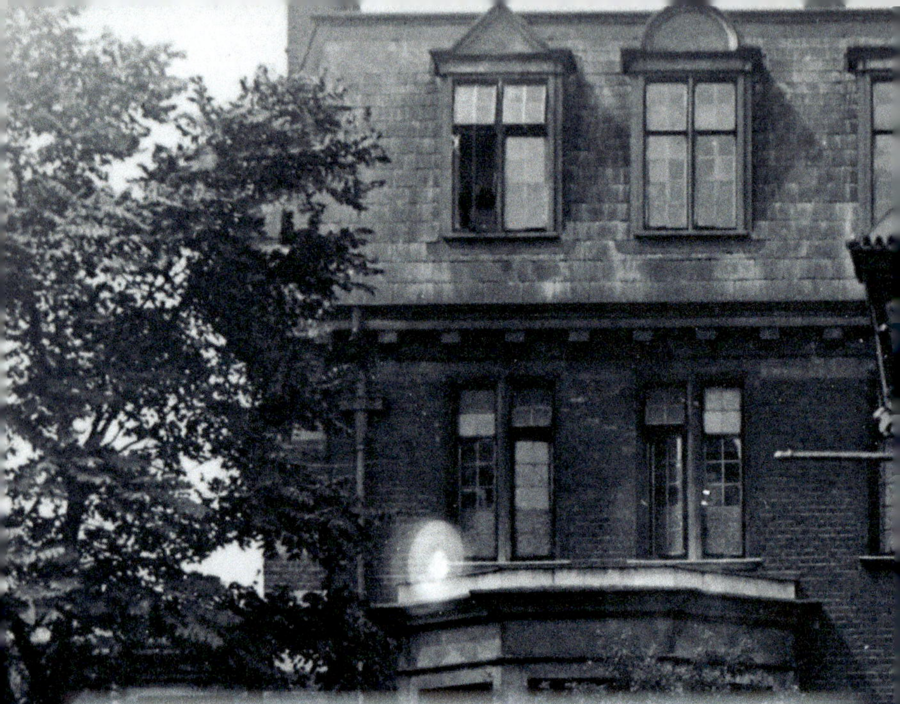

14. CARTER STREET POLICE STATION

Over 200 years ago, this was Keen's Row. Walworth House was its largest property, which had a long front garden. Subsequently, this was home to a Dr Carter, who later gave permission for Carter Street to be constructed on the land. Walworth House was later rebuilt but the garden was left and it can still be seen to this day from the top deck of any passing bus. The police service bought the lease in 1856 and it became Carter Street police station. In 1993 they moved to a modern purpose built station at Nos 12–28 Manor Place. The famous blue lamp from the aforementioned garden now stands outside the newly named Walworth Police Station.

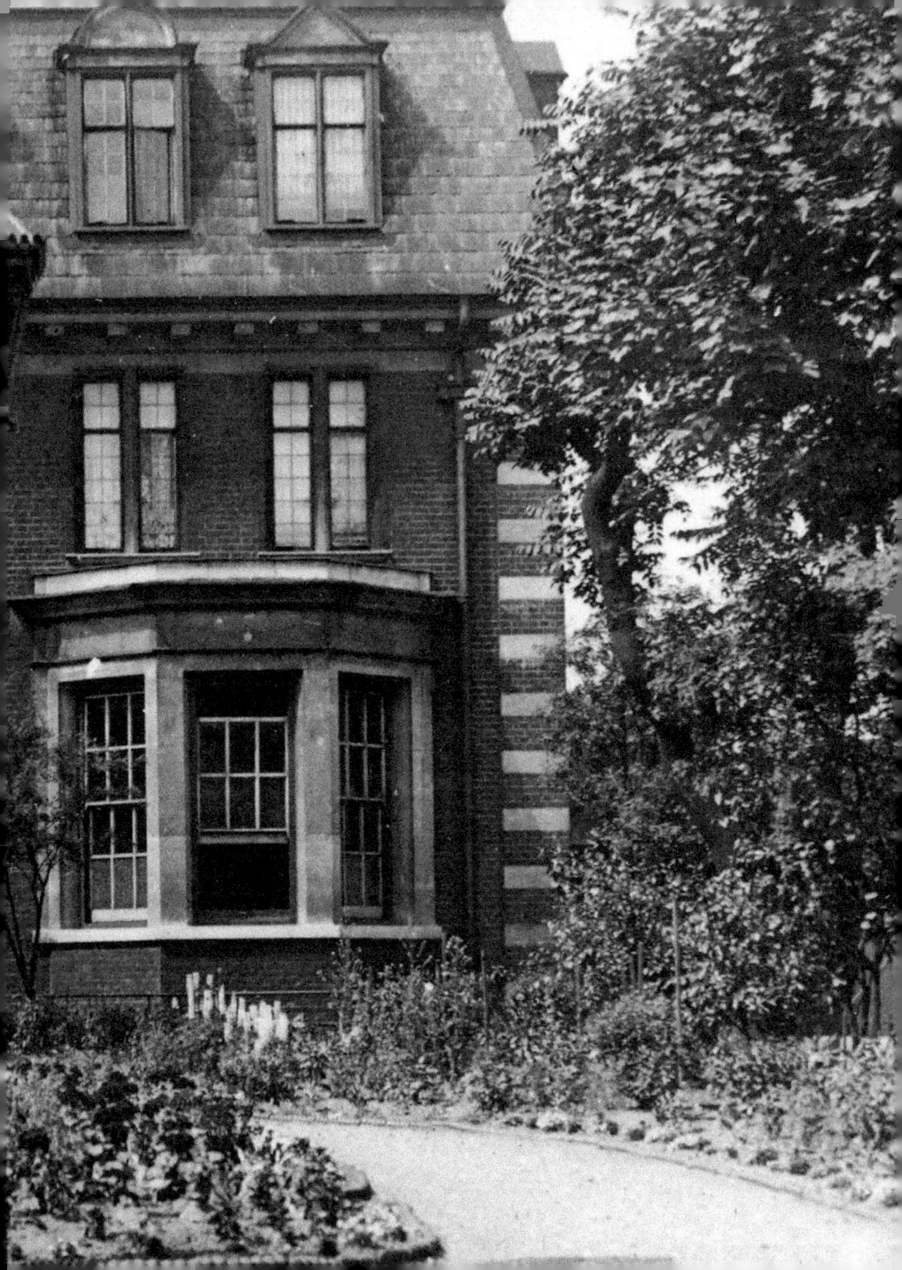

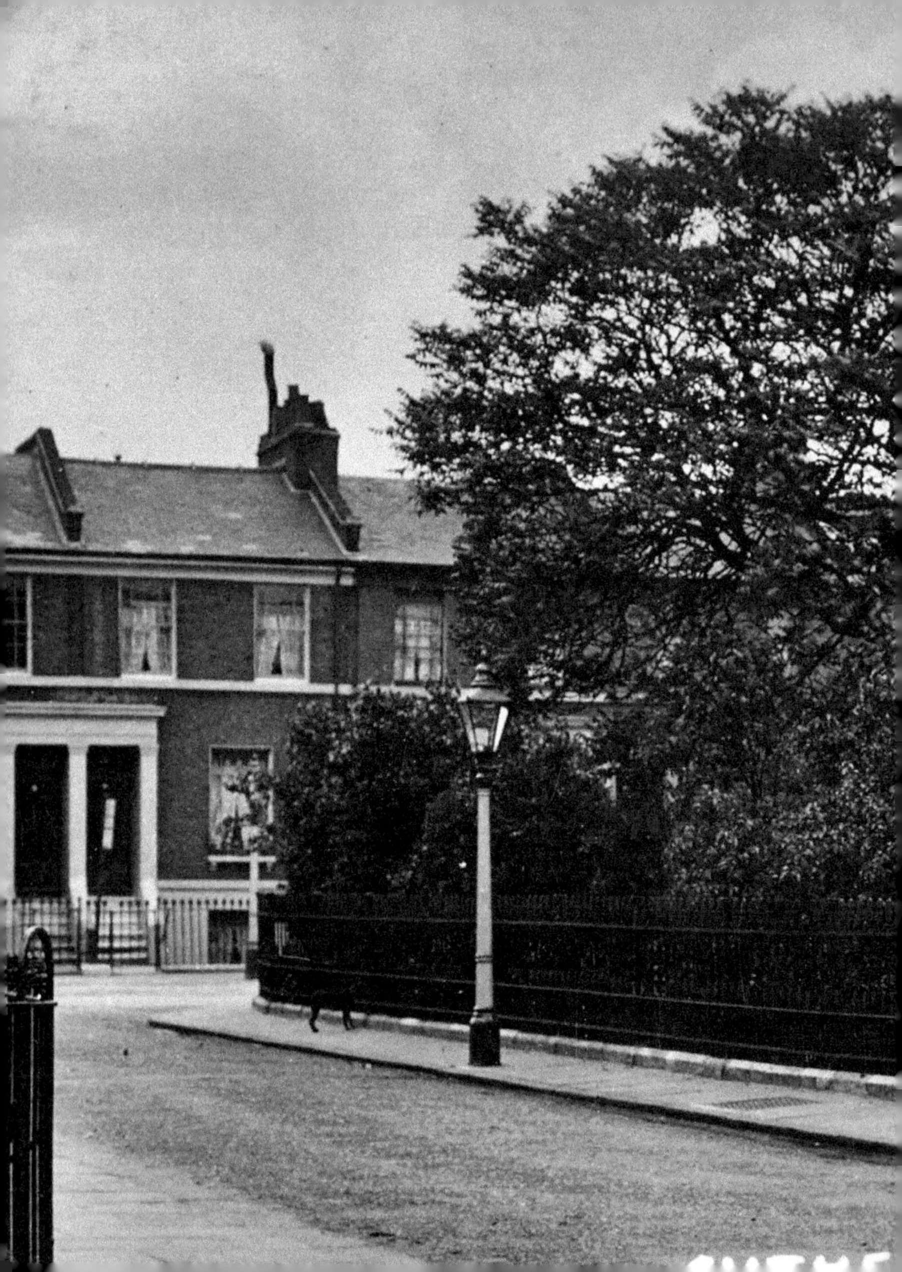

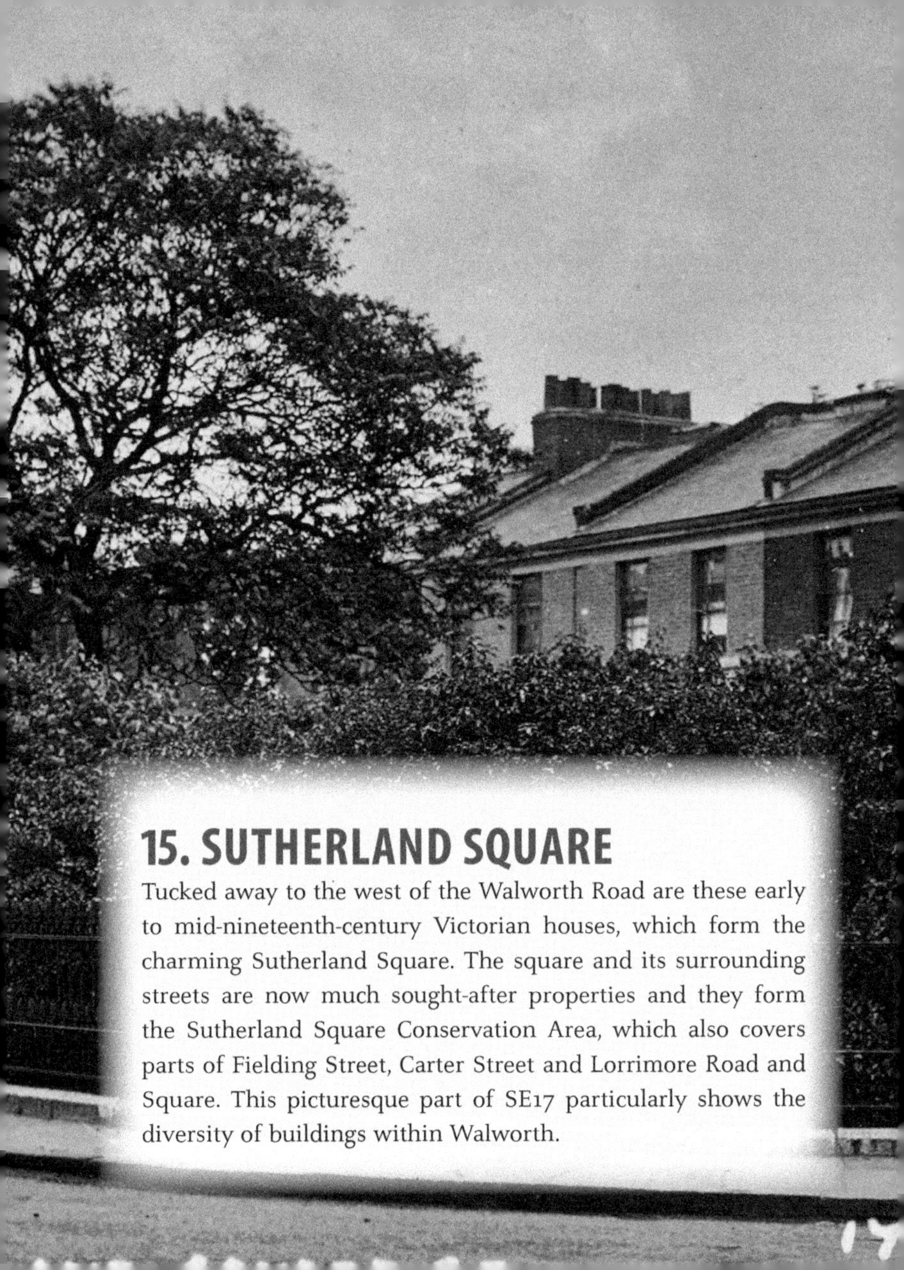

15. SUTHERLAND SQUARE

Tucked away to the west of the Walworth Road are these early to mid-nineteenth-century Victorian houses, which form the charming Sutherland Square. The square and its surrounding streets are now much sought-after properties and they form the Sutherland Square Conservation Area, which also covers parts of Fielding Street, Carter Street and Lorrimore Road and Square. This picturesque part of SE17 particularly shows the diversity of buildings within Walworth.

16. SHOPS, WALWORTH ROAD

Nothing highlights the passing of the years more clearly than the coming and goings of businesses on a high street. The Marks & Spencer double-fronted shop is a staple of the road, having first opened in 1914. Kennedy's closed in 2007 and the Grade II listed building currently has temporary tenants. Boots and Superdrug, while still trading on the road, have each moved premises since 1978, with Boots moving a few shops to the left and Superdrug moving into a much larger unit further right. Ravel is now Holland & Barrett and Dolland & Aitchison remains unmoved.

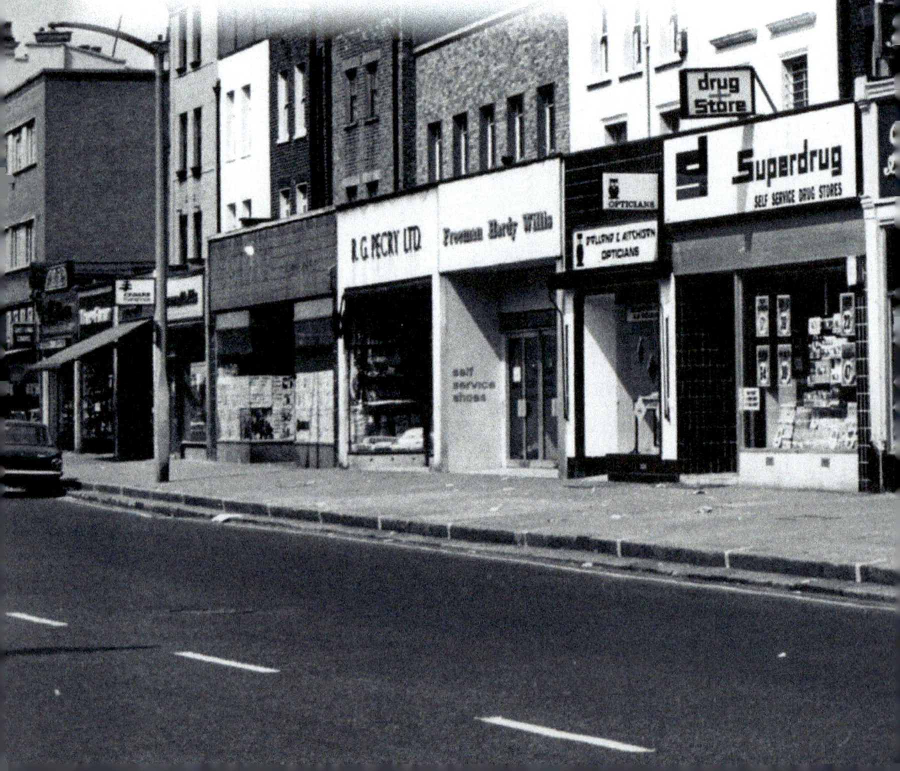

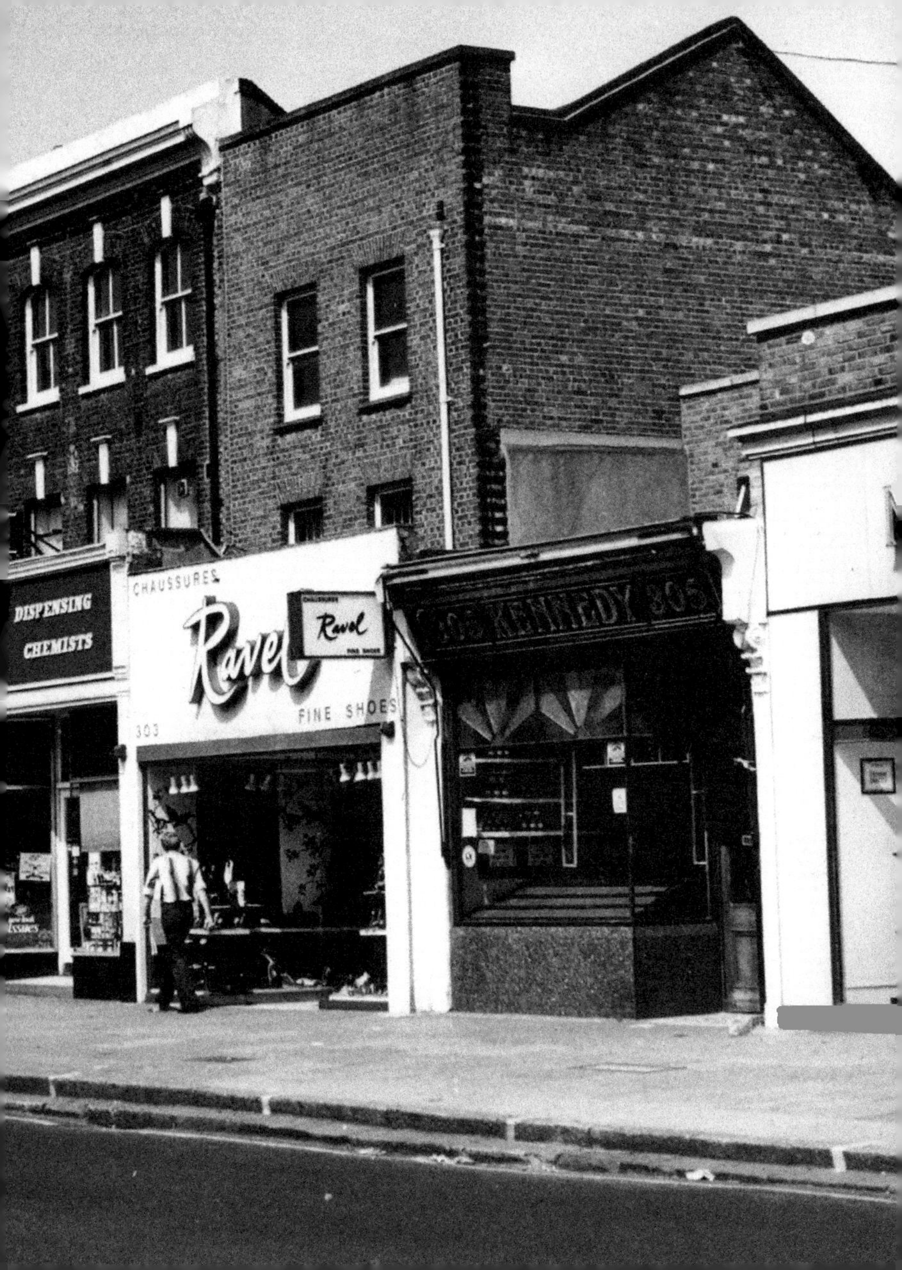
DISPENSING
CHEMISTS
CHAUSSURES
Ravel
Ravel
FINE SHOES
303
KENNEDY
305

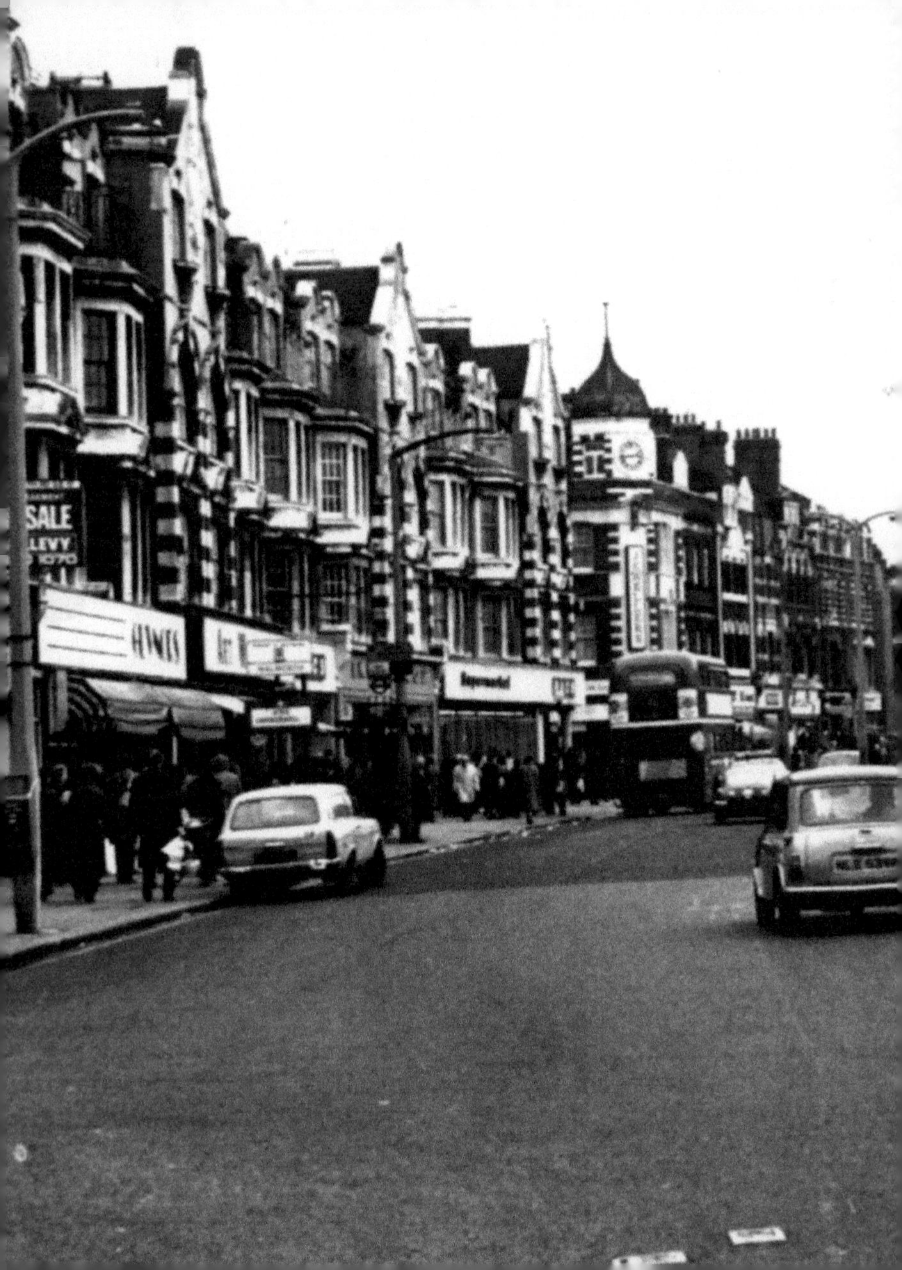
SALE
LEVY

17. SHOPS, WALWORTH ROAD

Looking back towards Camberwell, the highly ornate buildings from 1908 really stand out. Thankfully, they have survived and many are now private dwellings. To the right of is the old Co-operative store. To the left is Guvnors, a popular gentleman's fashion shop, and Art Wallpapers. Bet Fred the bookmakers, The clock on top of the old Harvey & Thompson jewellers and pawnbrokers can still be seen today.

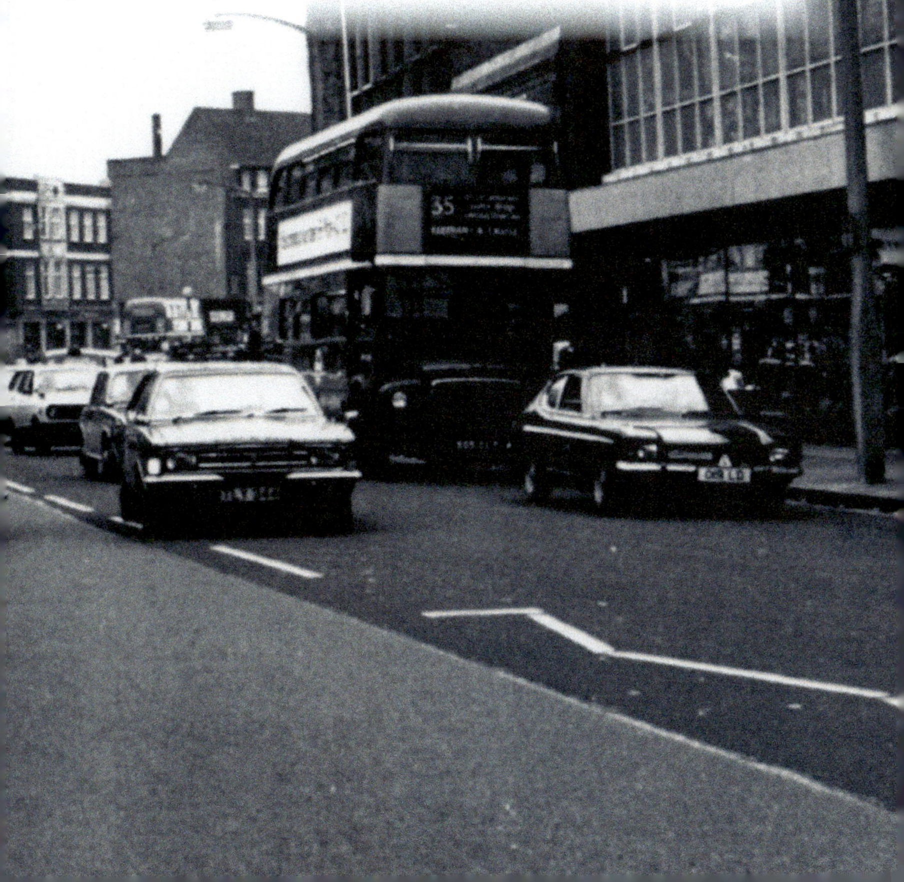

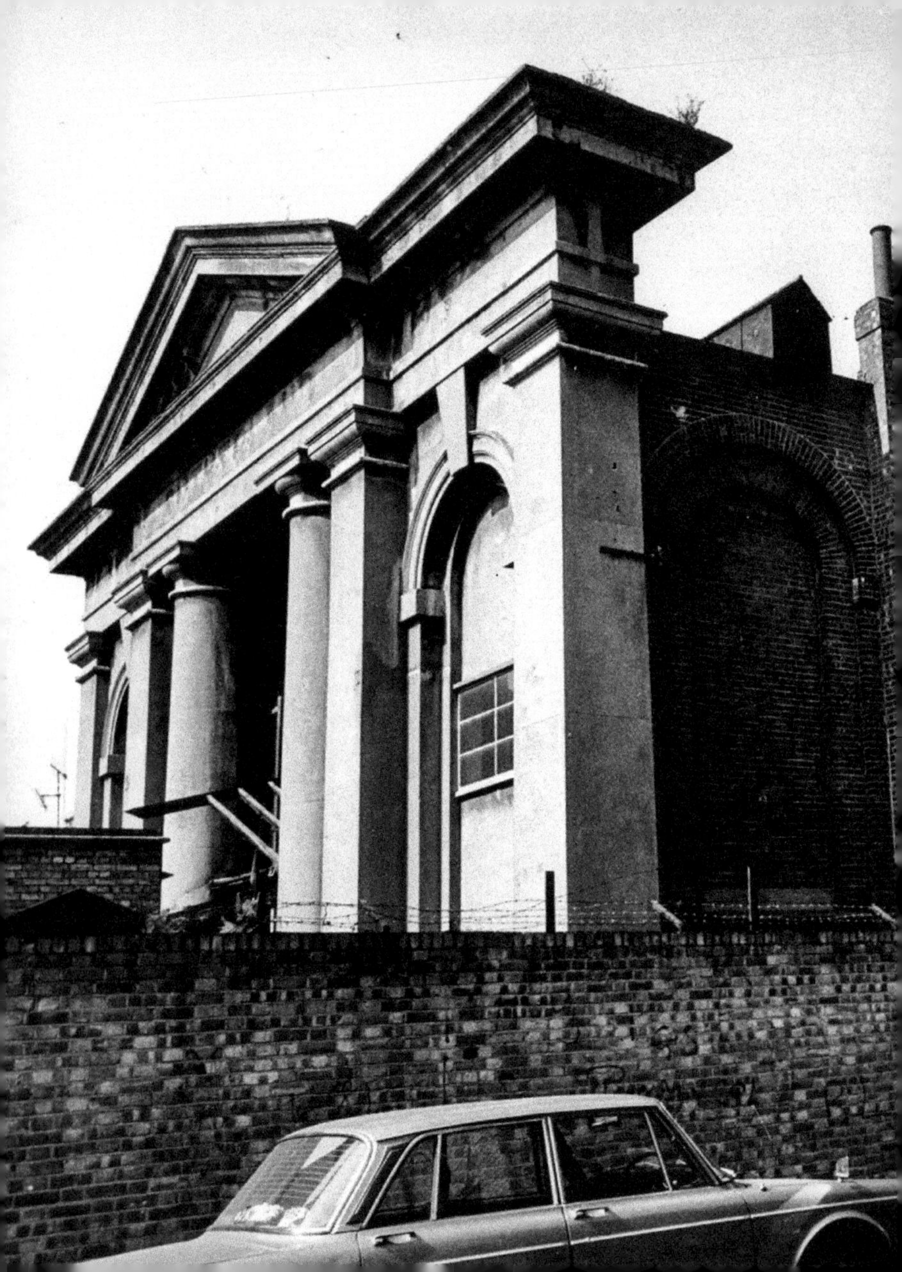

18. SUTHERLAND CHAPEL

Built in 1842 between St Peter's church in Liverpool Grove and the Walworth Road, this Congregational chapel was intended for Dr Edward Andrews, the minister at the nearby Beresford Street Chapel (Beresford Street was renamed John Ruskin Street in 1937). However, Andrews died before the chapel was completed and the Revd John Wood became its first minister. Sutherland chapel closed in 1904 and became the Electric Theatre Co., the first 'picture palace' in Walworth, which seated on the original pews 780 paying customers. Later it became a storage space for a theatrical company and was then developed for luxury housing and is today known as Malvern House. The original façade of the chapel can still be seen directly behind the shop 'Art and Magic' at Nos 343–345 Walworth Road.

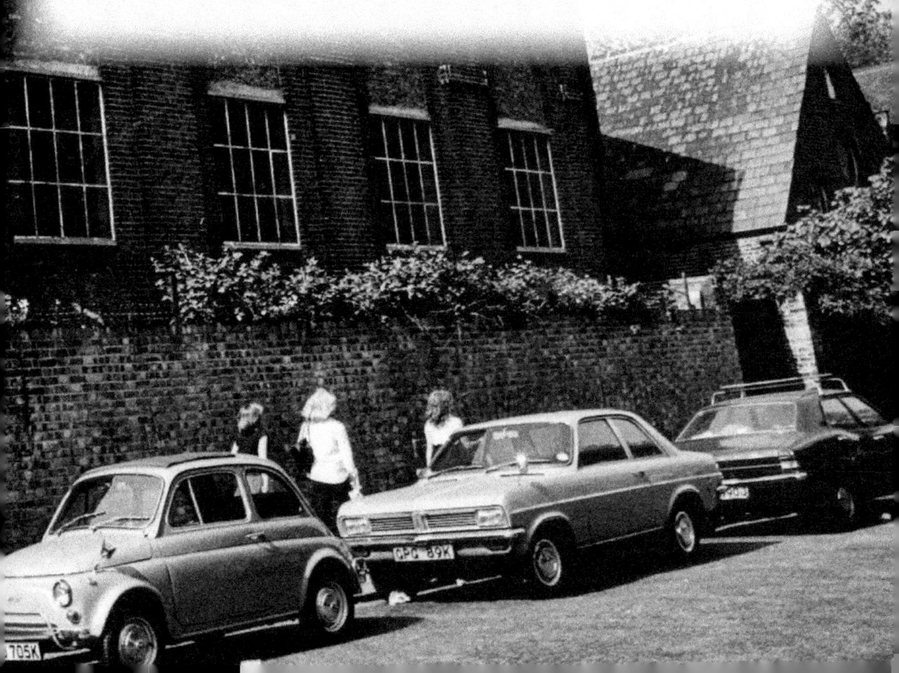

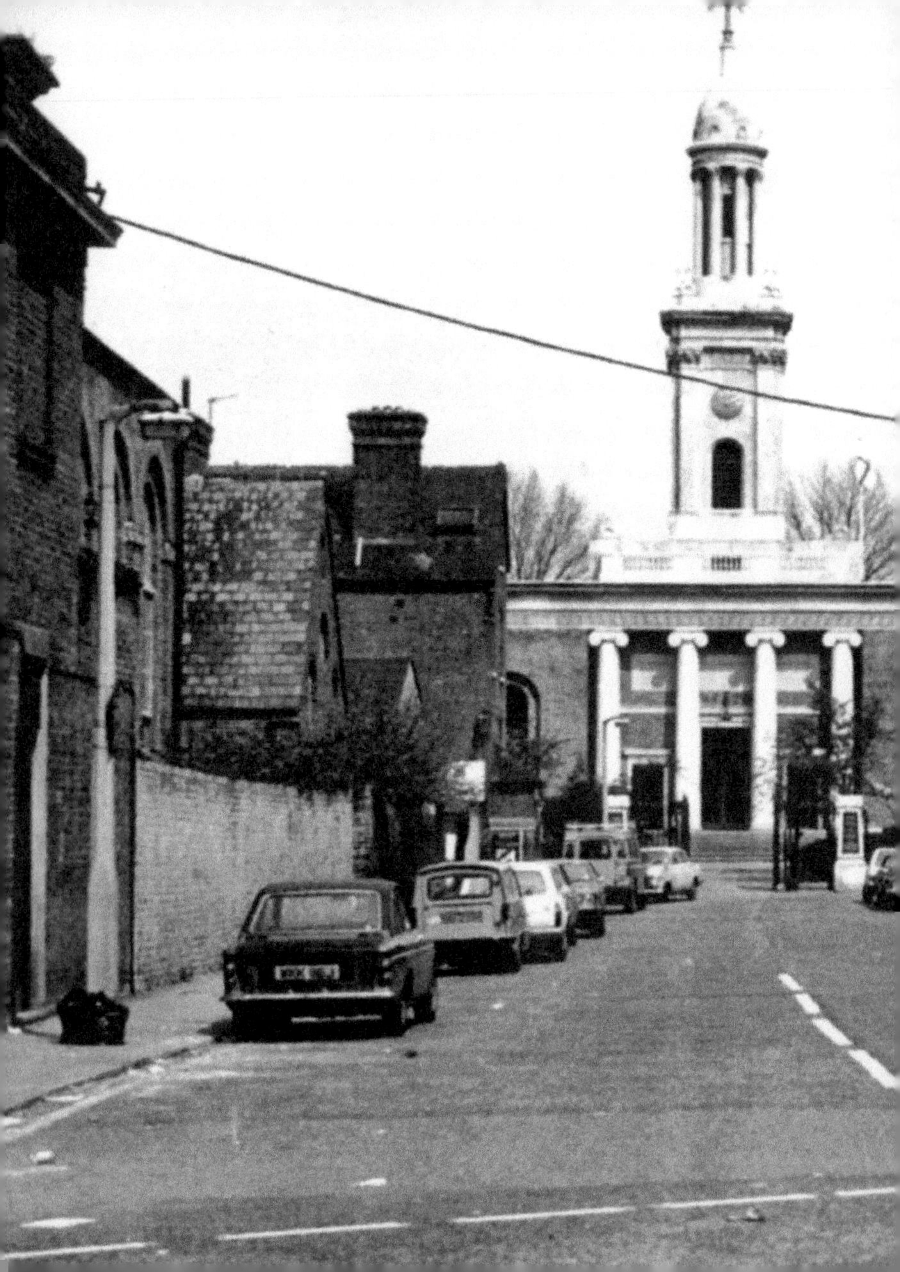

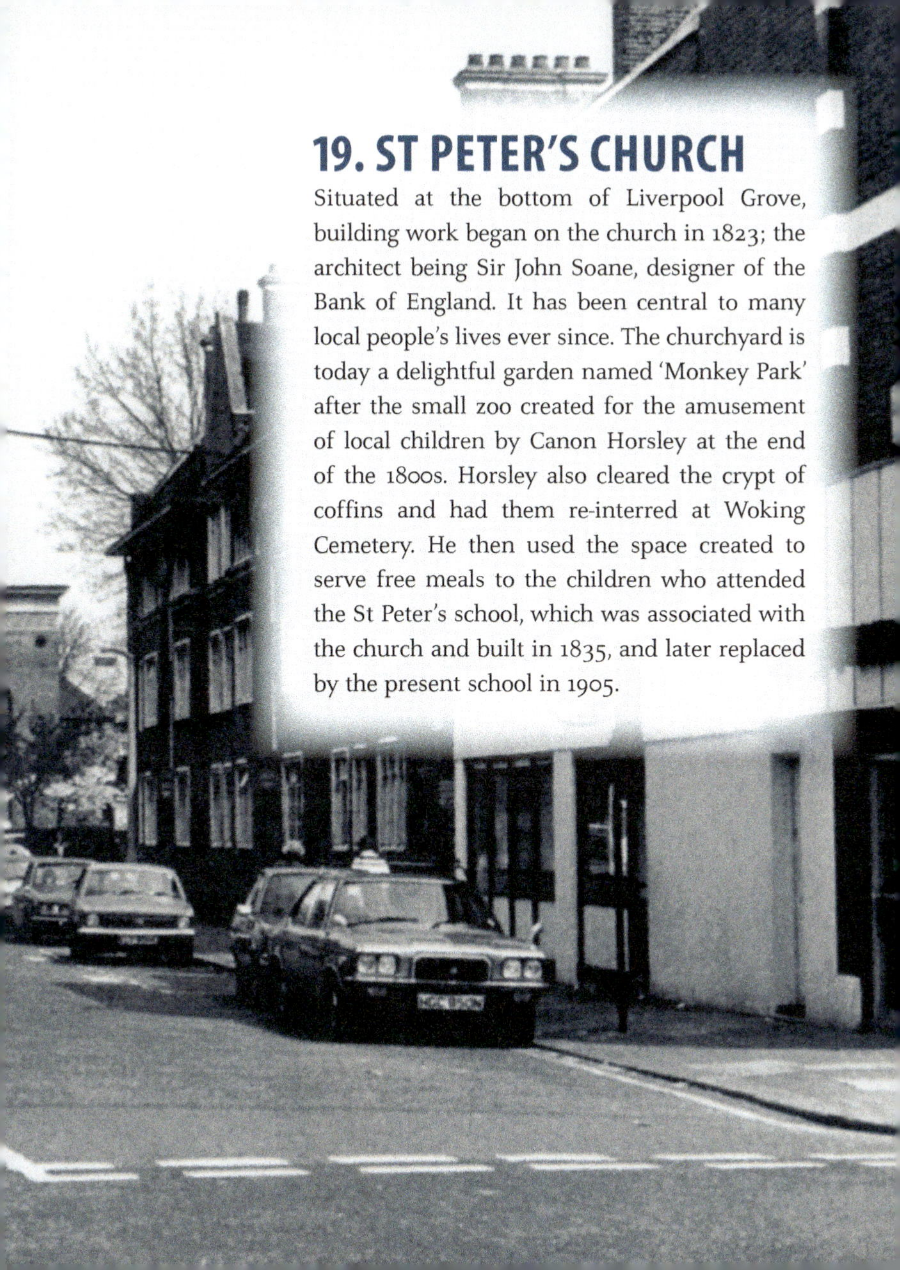

19. ST PETER'S CHURCH

Situated at the bottom of Liverpool Grove, building work began on the church in 1823; the architect being Sir John Soane, designer of the Bank of England. It has been central to many local people's lives ever since. The churchyard is today a delightful garden named 'Monkey Park' after the small zoo created for the amusement of local children by Canon Horsley at the end of the 1800s. Horsley also cleared the crypt of coffins and had them re-interred at Woking Cemetery. He then used the space created to serve free meals to the children who attended the St Peter's school, which was associated with the church and built in 1835, and later replaced by the present school in 1905.

20. FARADAY GARDENS

This local swing park is named after scientist Michael Faraday (1791–1867), who was born in Newington Butts. His work led to the successful development of electro-mechanical machinery, which came to dominate heavy industry in the nineteenth century. An air-raid shelter was built here during the Second World War and could house up to 600 people. The Broadmayne and Woodsford housing blocks here were erected in 1965.

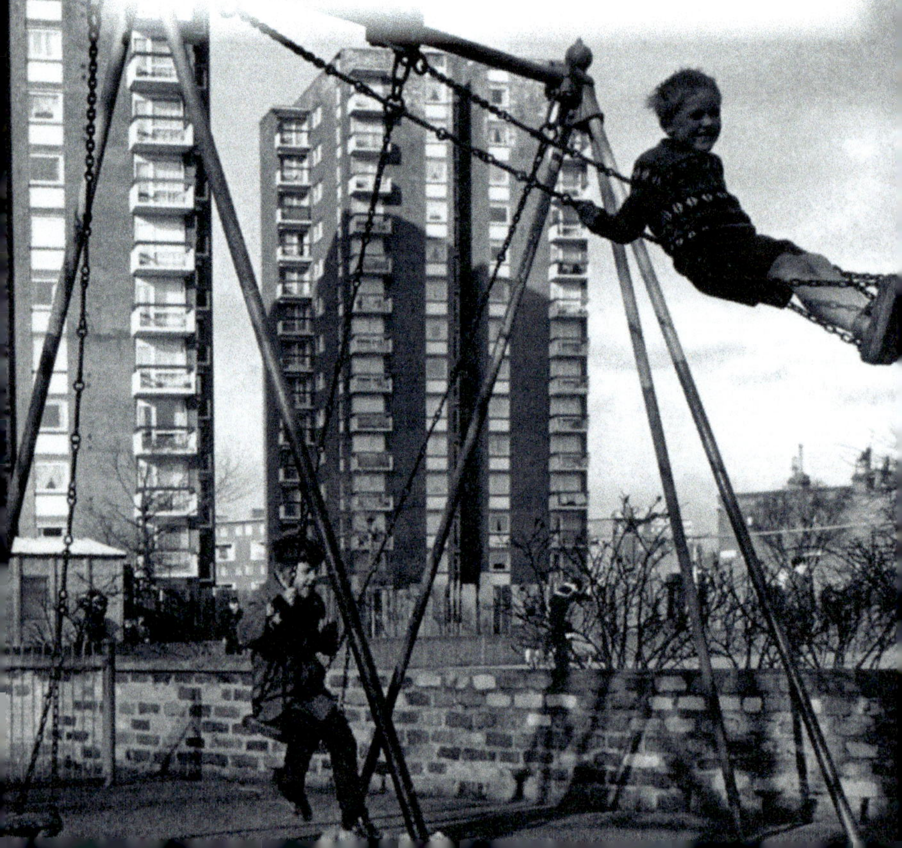

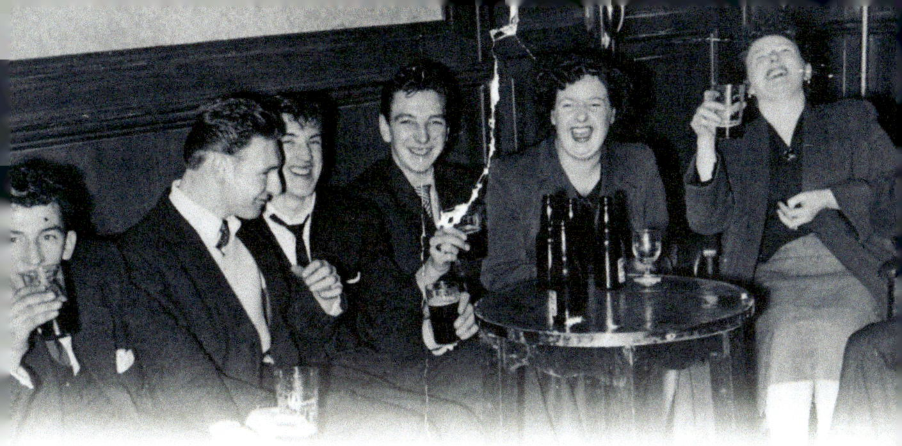

21. TEMPLE BAR

Situated at Nos 284–286, the mock Tudor frontage is a familiar site on the Walworth Road. In 1949 the pub was used as an art gallery by the artist and occult magician Austin Osman Spare, who had exhibited at the Royal Academy in 1904 at the tender age of seventeen. For a month, Spare's idiosyncratic paintings and drawings hung in the pub. The views of the pub locals on the surrealist pop art-style artwork sadly aren't recorded.

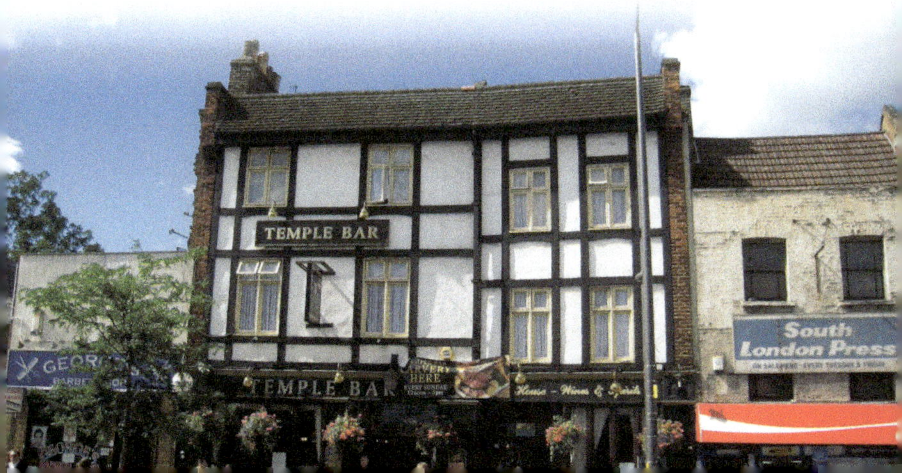

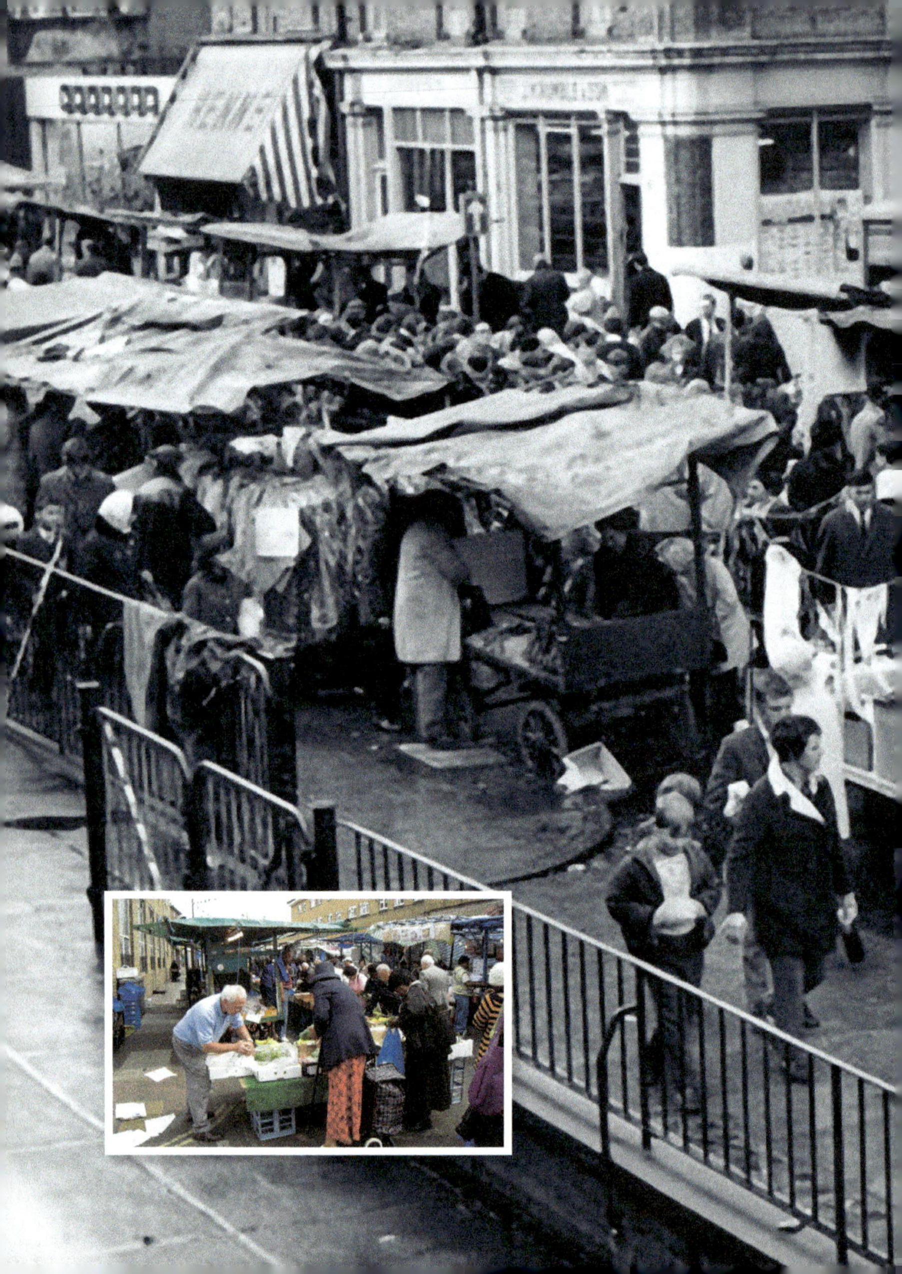

22. EAST STREET MARKET

Known locally as 'The Lane', this market has been at the heart of the area since it officially started trading in 1880. However, there are reports of street selling in Walworth going back to the sixteenth century and stalls lined the Walworth Road right up until the late 1800s. Gradually, the traders were eased into East Street when tramlines were laid in 1871. In the early days of the market, no pitch was guaranteed and traders had to wait in the side streets for a policeman to blow his whistle at 8.30 a.m. before they could rush out and construct their stalls. Regular pitches began in 1927. The vast majority of the traders were local people who lived in the back streets that surrounded the market. And their customers came from the same streets too as few people could afford to travel too far from home.

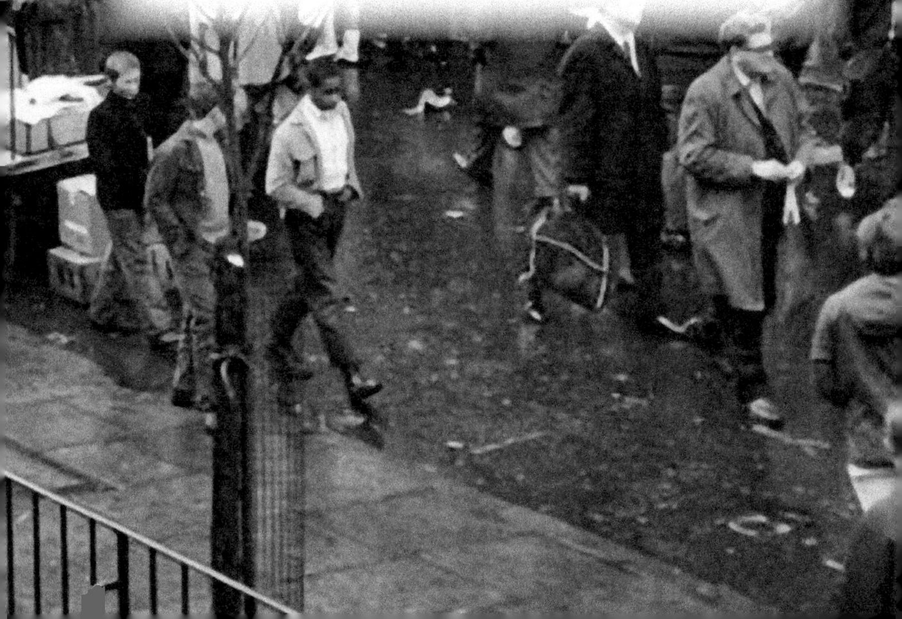

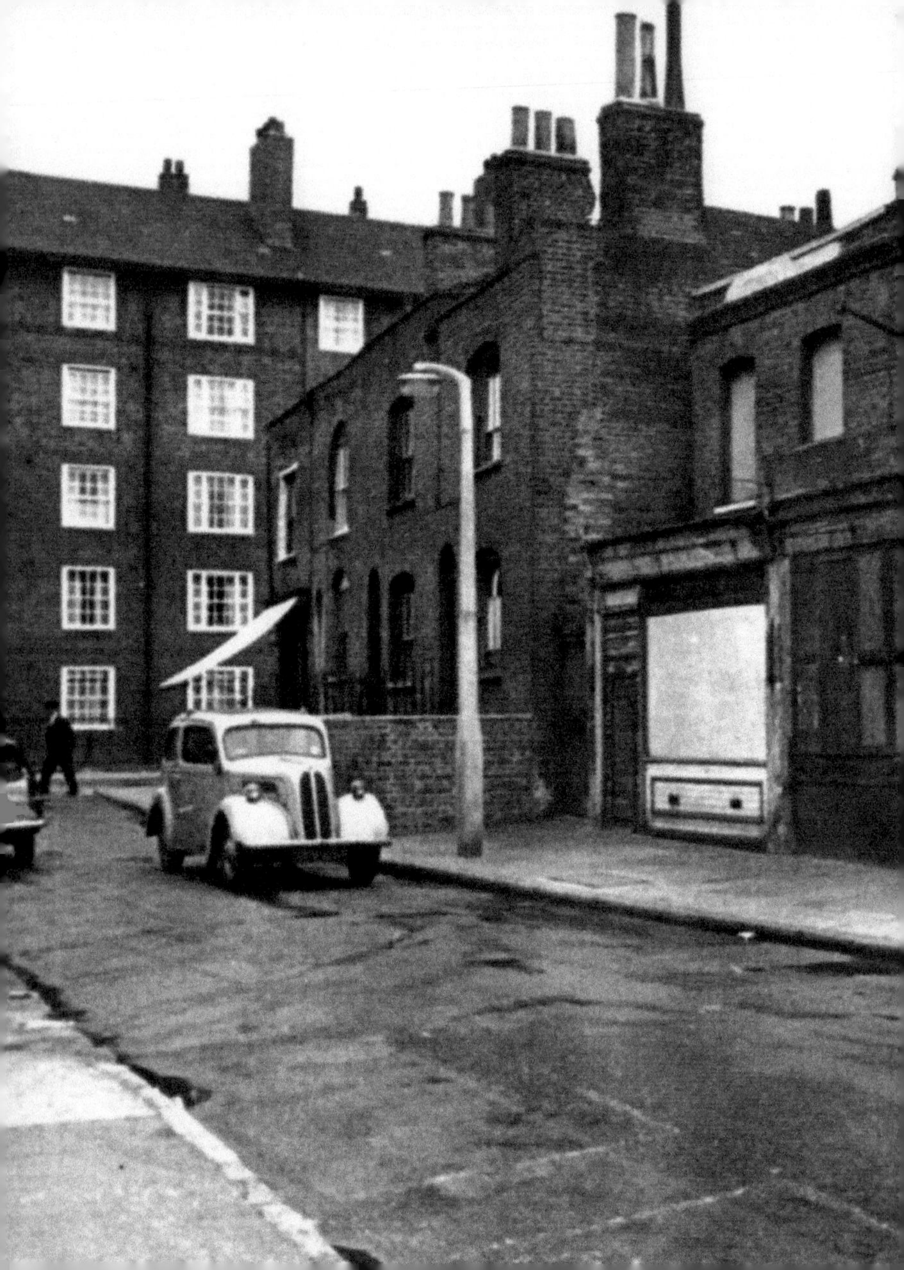

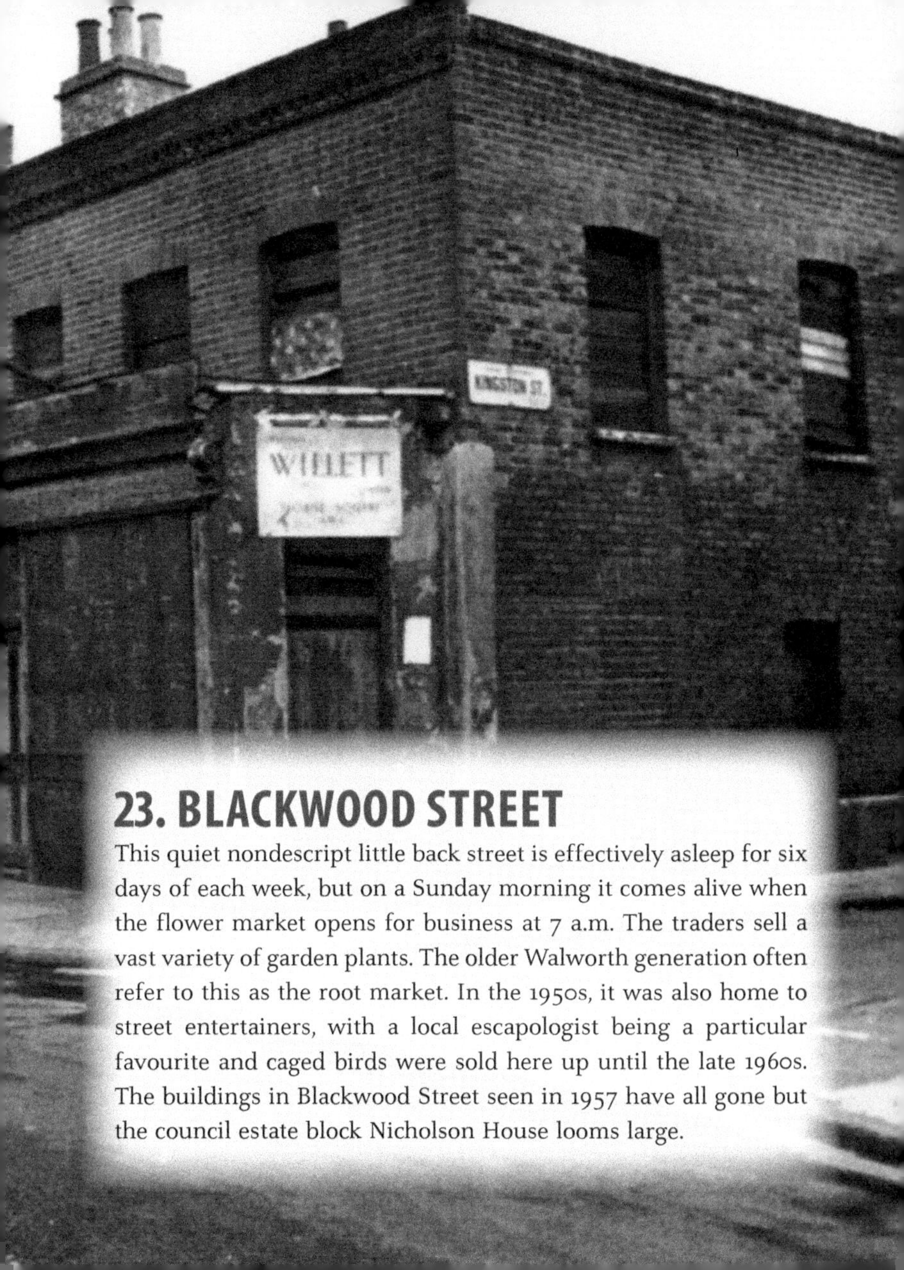

23. BLACKWOOD STREET

This quiet nondescript little back street is effectively asleep for six days of each week, but on a Sunday morning it comes alive when the flower market opens for business at 7 a.m. The traders sell a vast variety of garden plants. The older Walworth generation often refer to this as the root market. In the 1950s, it was also home to street entertainers, with a local escapologist being a particular favourite and caged birds were sold here up until the late 1960s. The buildings in Blackwood Street seen in 1957 have all gone but the council estate block Nicholson House looms large.

24. EAST STREET BAPTIST CHURCH

At the rear of the building a stone plaque identifies it as once being the Richmond Street Mission and Ragged School opened in 1859. Princess Christian, daughter of Queen Victoria and Prince Albert, laid the foundation stone of the church on this site in 1896. Situated at No. 177 East Street on the corner of Portland Street, and once known as the East Street Mission, the church is still in use averaging a congregation of fifty people on most Sundays.

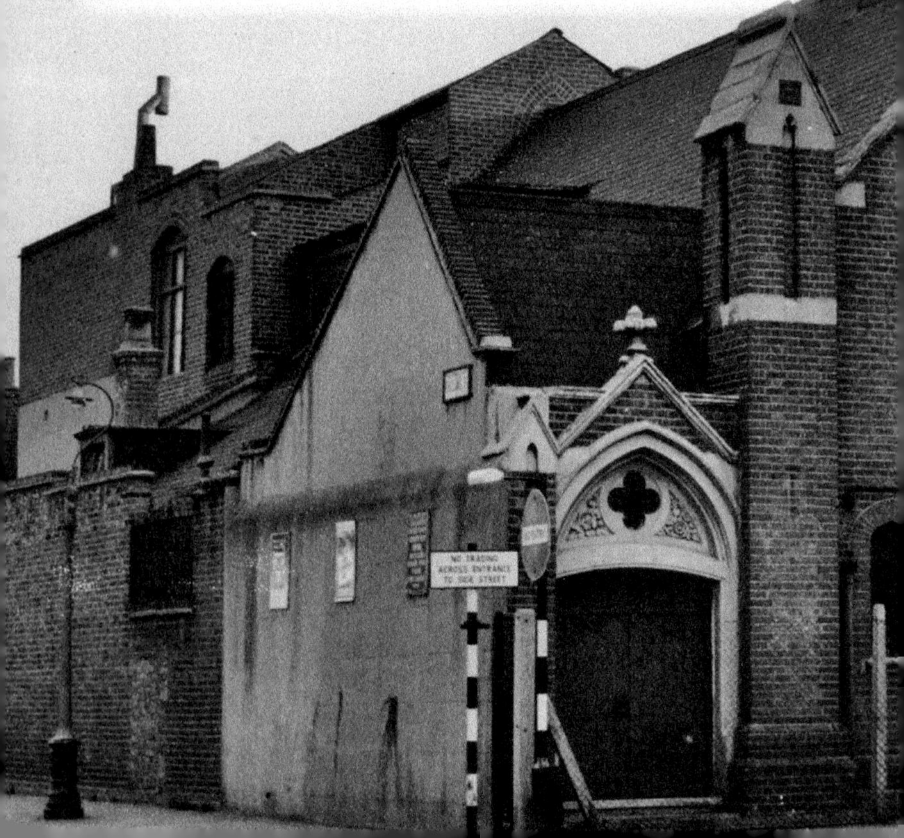

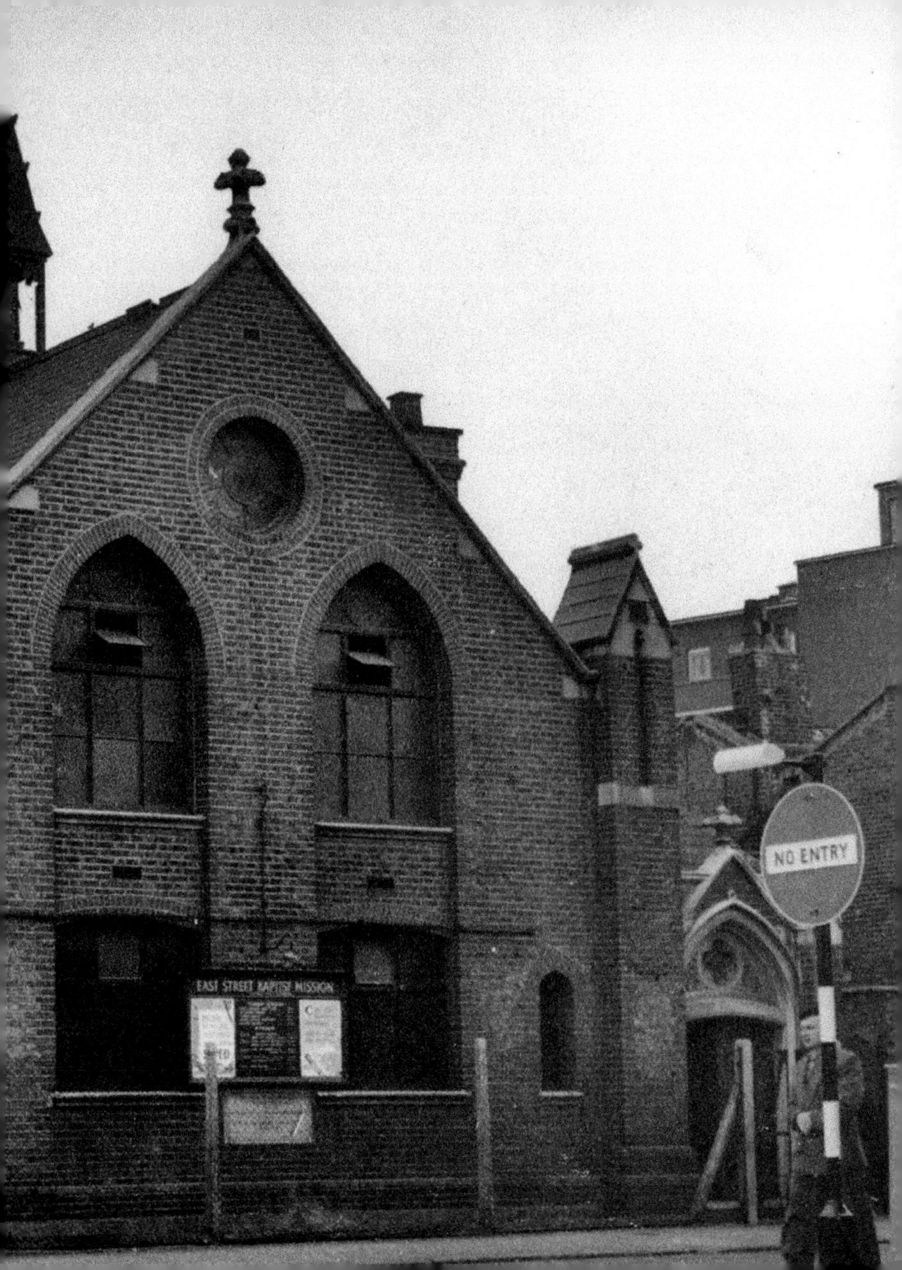
EAST STREET BAPTIST MISSION
NO ENTRY

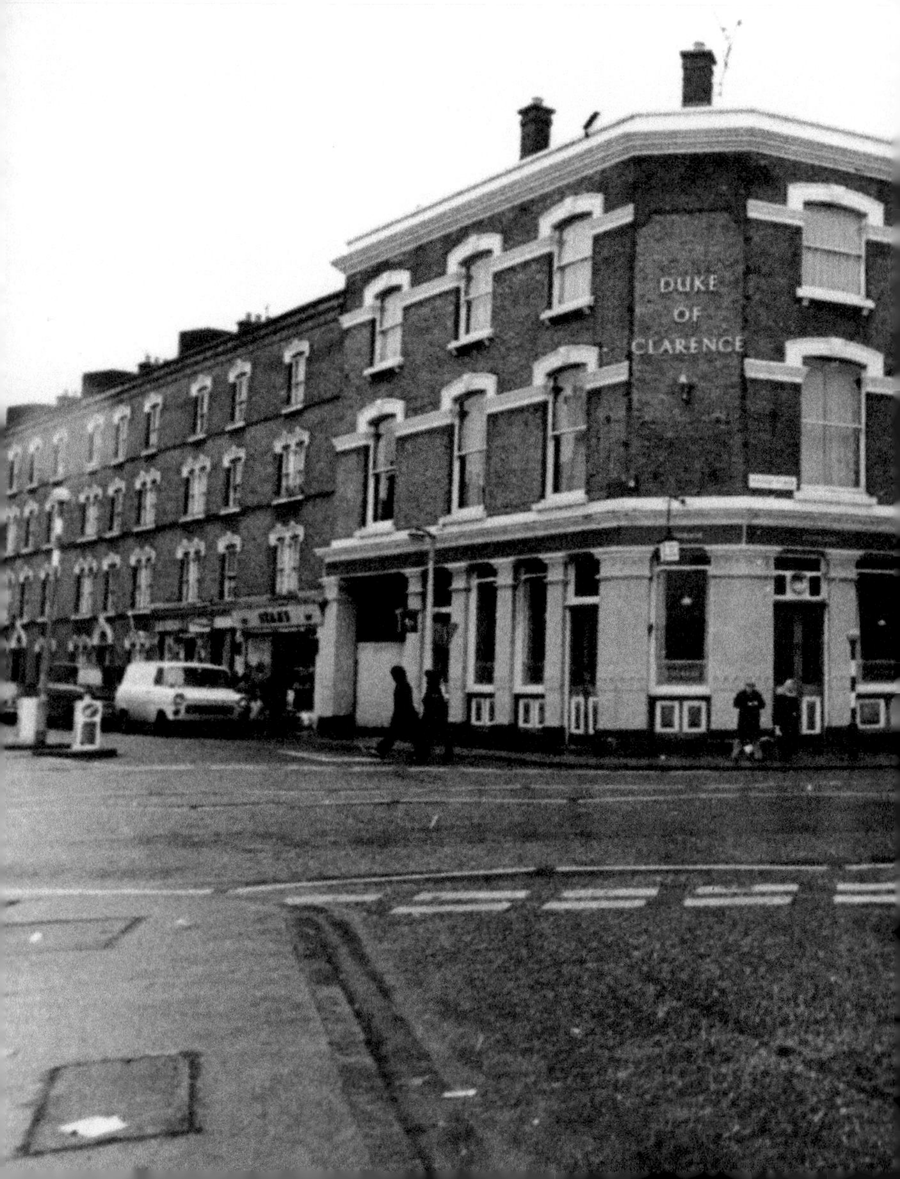
DUKE
OF
CLARENCE

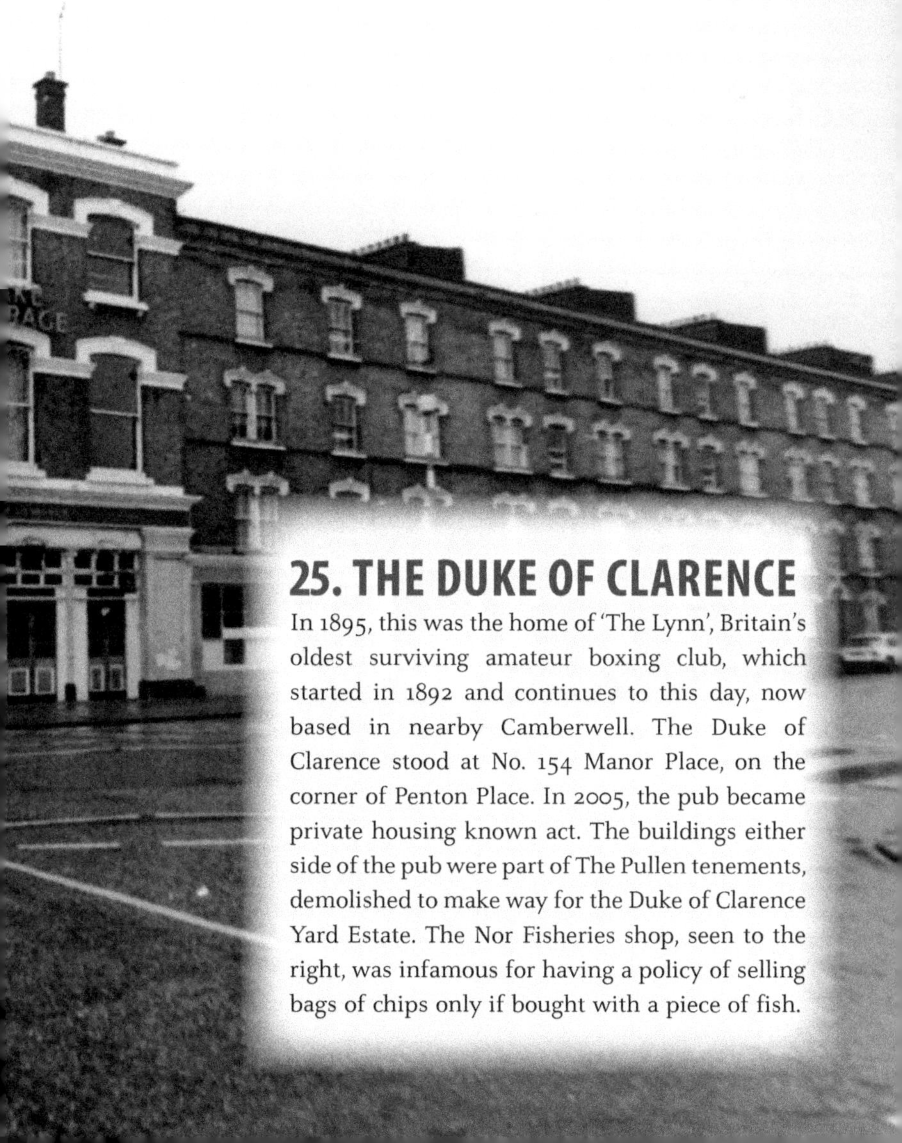

25. THE DUKE OF CLARENCE

In 1895, this was the home of 'The Lynn', Britain's oldest surviving amateur boxing club, which started in 1892 and continues to this day, now based in nearby Camberwell. The Duke of Clarence stood at No. 154 Manor Place, on the corner of Penton Place. In 2005, the pub became private housing known act. The buildings either side of the pub were part of The Pullen tenements, demolished to make way for the Duke of Clarence Yard Estate. The Nor Fisheries shop, seen to the right, was infamous for having a policy of selling bags of chips only if bought with a piece of fish.

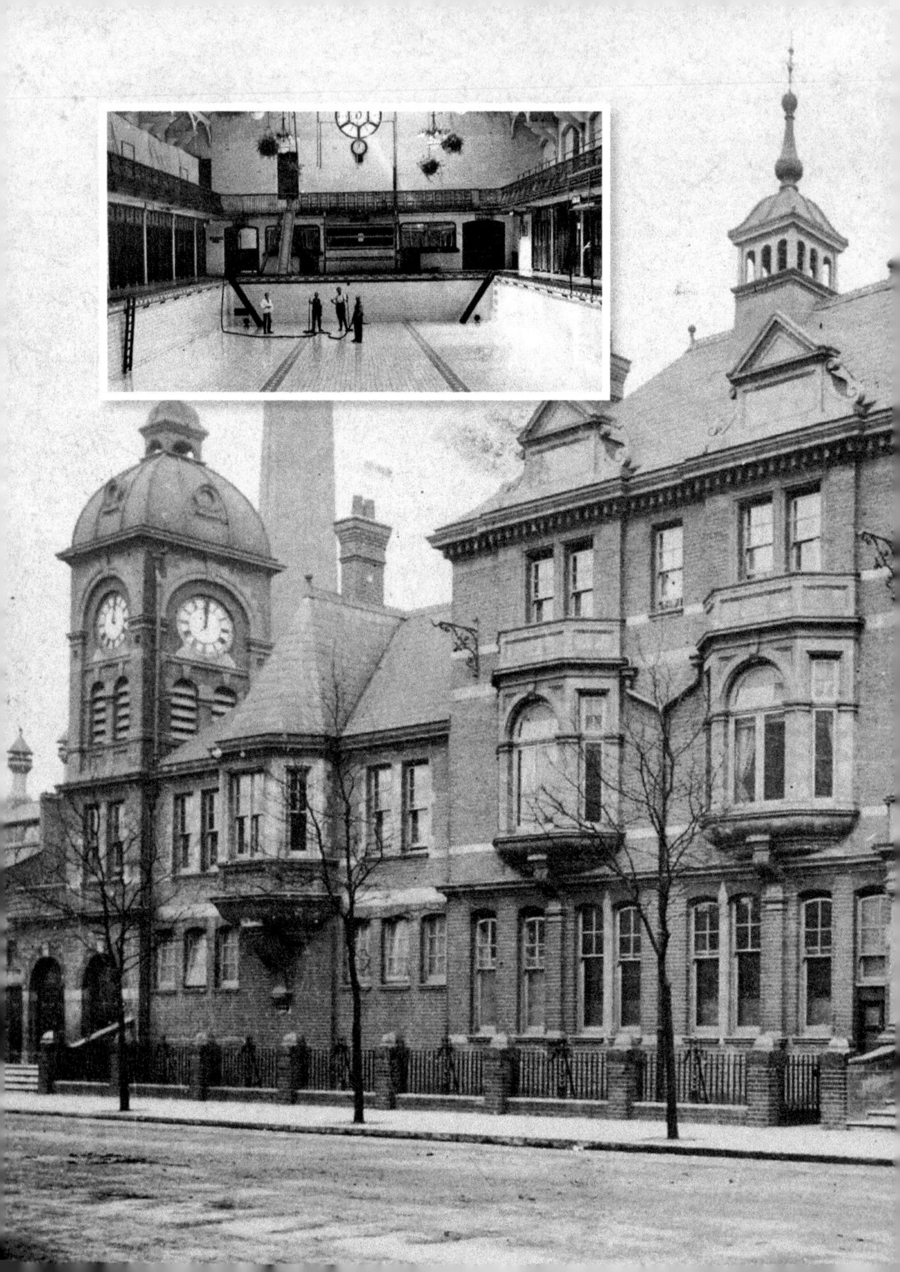

26. MANOR PLACE BATHS

This Grade II listed building was opened on 16 March 1898 built at a cost of £60,000 from a design by E. B. I'Anson. It contained a public washhouse, a laundry and swimming baths. Generations of Walworth residents used the facilities, encouraged to do so to maintain personal hygiene. As well as a swimming venue, the halls were used for civic and social functions as well as staging other sporting occasions with boxing particularly popular, both amateur and professional.

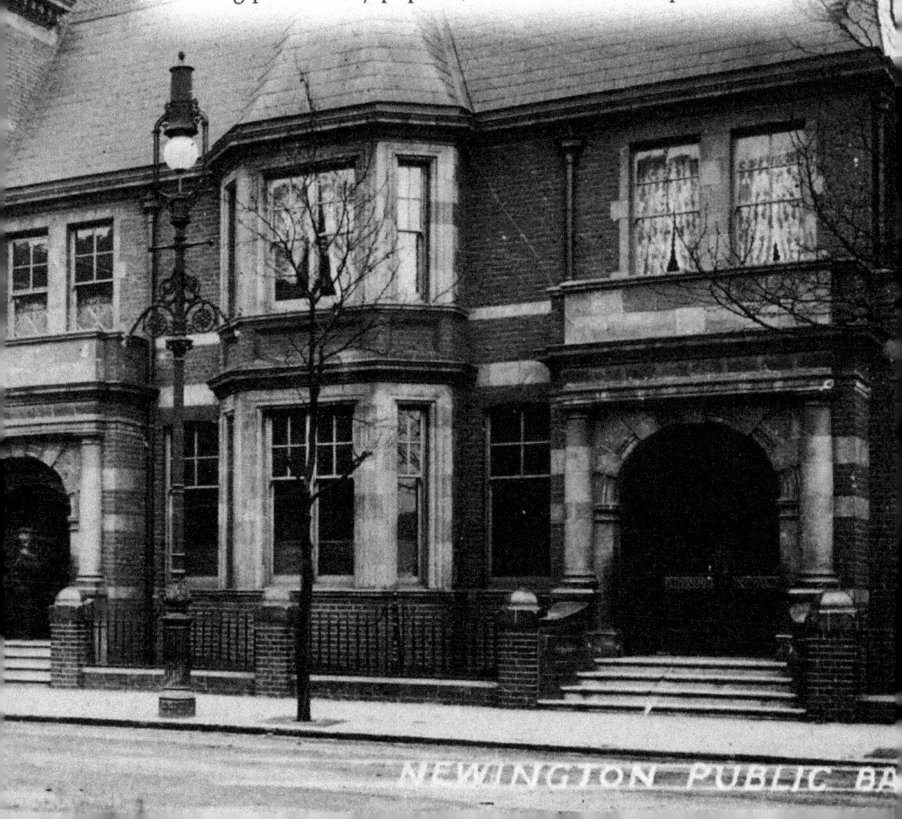

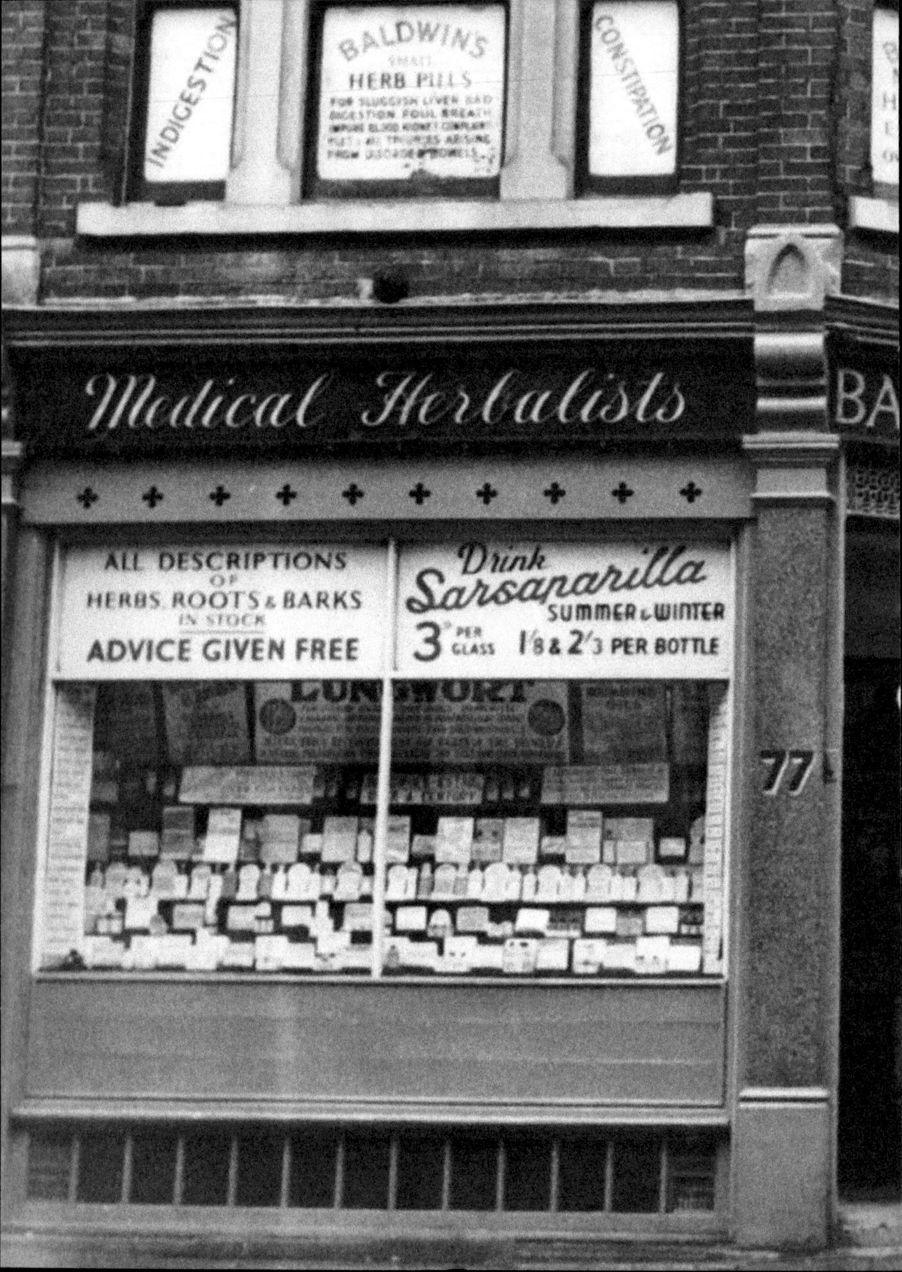
INDIGESTION
BALDWIN'S
SMALL
HERB PILLS
CONSTIPATION
Medical Herbalists
ALL DESCRIPTIONS
OF
HERBS, ROOTS & BARKS
IN STOCK
ADVICE GIVEN FREE
Drink
Sarsaparilla
SUMMER & WINTER
3d PER GLASS
1/8 & 2/3 PER BOTTLE
77

27. G. BALDWIN & CO.

G. Baldwin & Co. is London's oldest and most established herbalist. The company was founded by George Baldwin in 1844 here we see the original shop at No. 77 Walworth Road. In 1918, Henry Dagnell joined the company. His role was to restore the failing G. Baldwin business, which he did, leading him to eventually buy the company. In 1969, Baldwin's was forced by development work on the vast Heygate Estate to relocate to No. 173 Walworth Road where they are still based today. In 1978, they bought No. 171 next door, and combined both buildings.

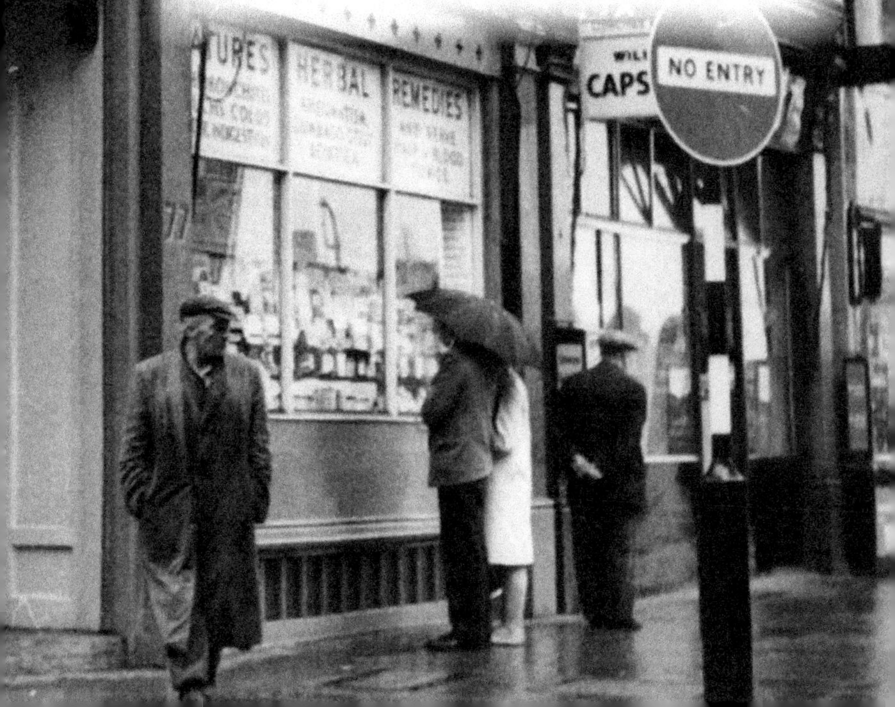

28. ST MARK'S CHURCH HALL

This lovely little building was the parish hall of St Mark's church, which was designed by Henry Jarvis in 1874. Enemy bombing in the Second World War destroyed the church. The hall once had a viewing balcony and its original stone font can be found at the rear of the building. The building has been the Chapel Furnishers store for the past twenty-four years.

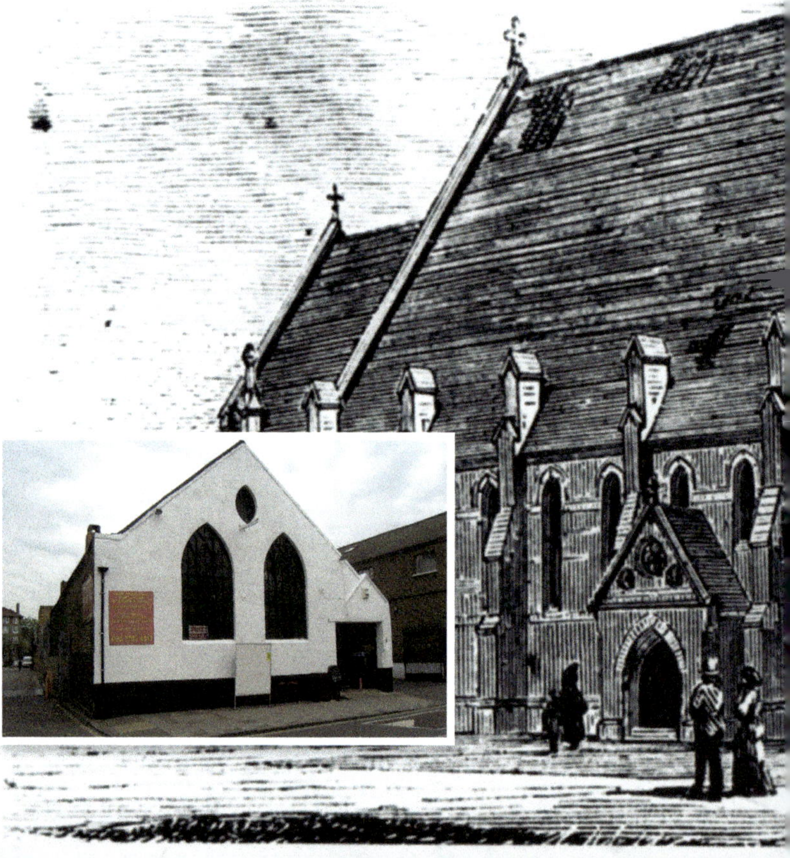

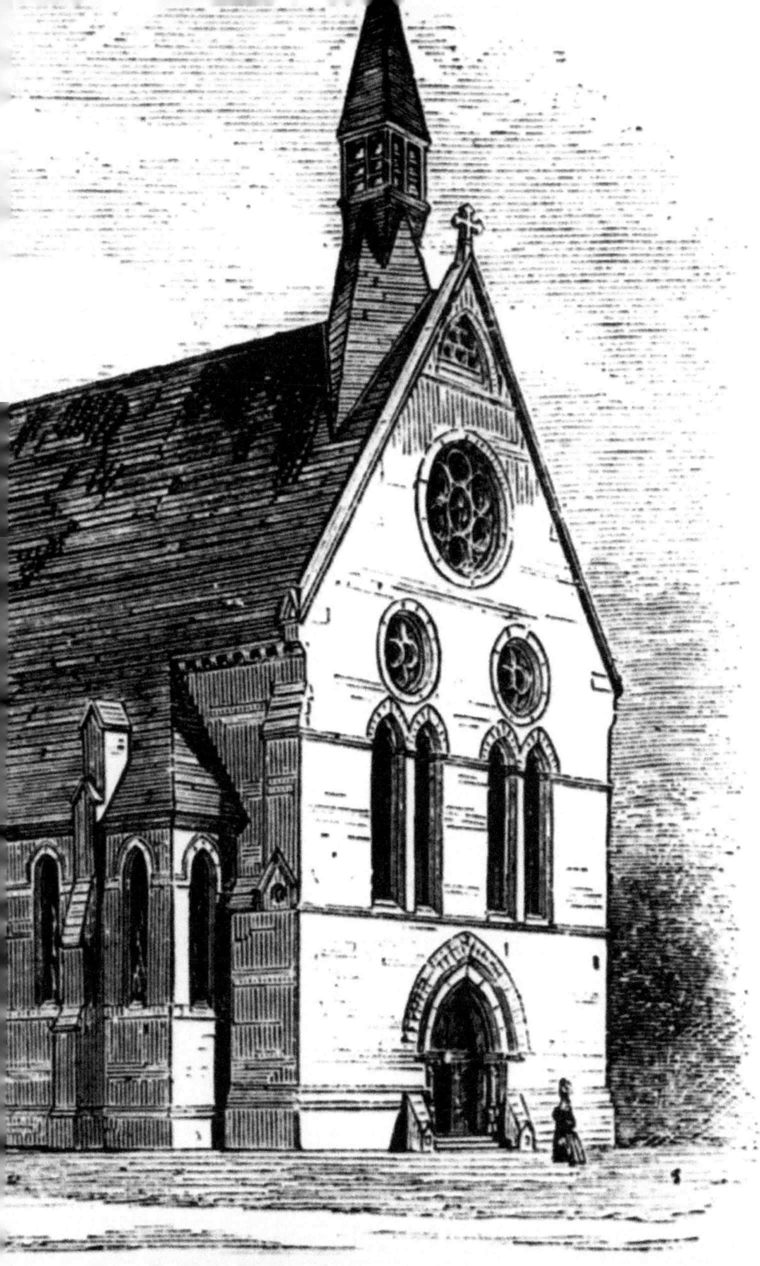

29. PULLENS BUILDINGS

Local builder James Pullen & Son built the estate over fifteen years from 1886 to 1901. A couple of the original twelve blocks were destroyed in the Second World War, others demolished to make way for new housing estates during the 1970s. The surviving buildings are some of the last remaining Victorian tenements in London and now form part of a conservation area. In 1899, the tenants paid 8 shillings per week for three rooms, which included a scullery and a kitchen. An extra 6 pennies were charged for the gas supply and cleaning of the stairs. Ground-floor properties had access to the work yards that adjoined the buildings. In the late 1970s Southwark Council planned to demolish the rest of the buildings, but a combination of existing residents and squatters fought a campaign to save them. Around half of the flats are now privately owned.

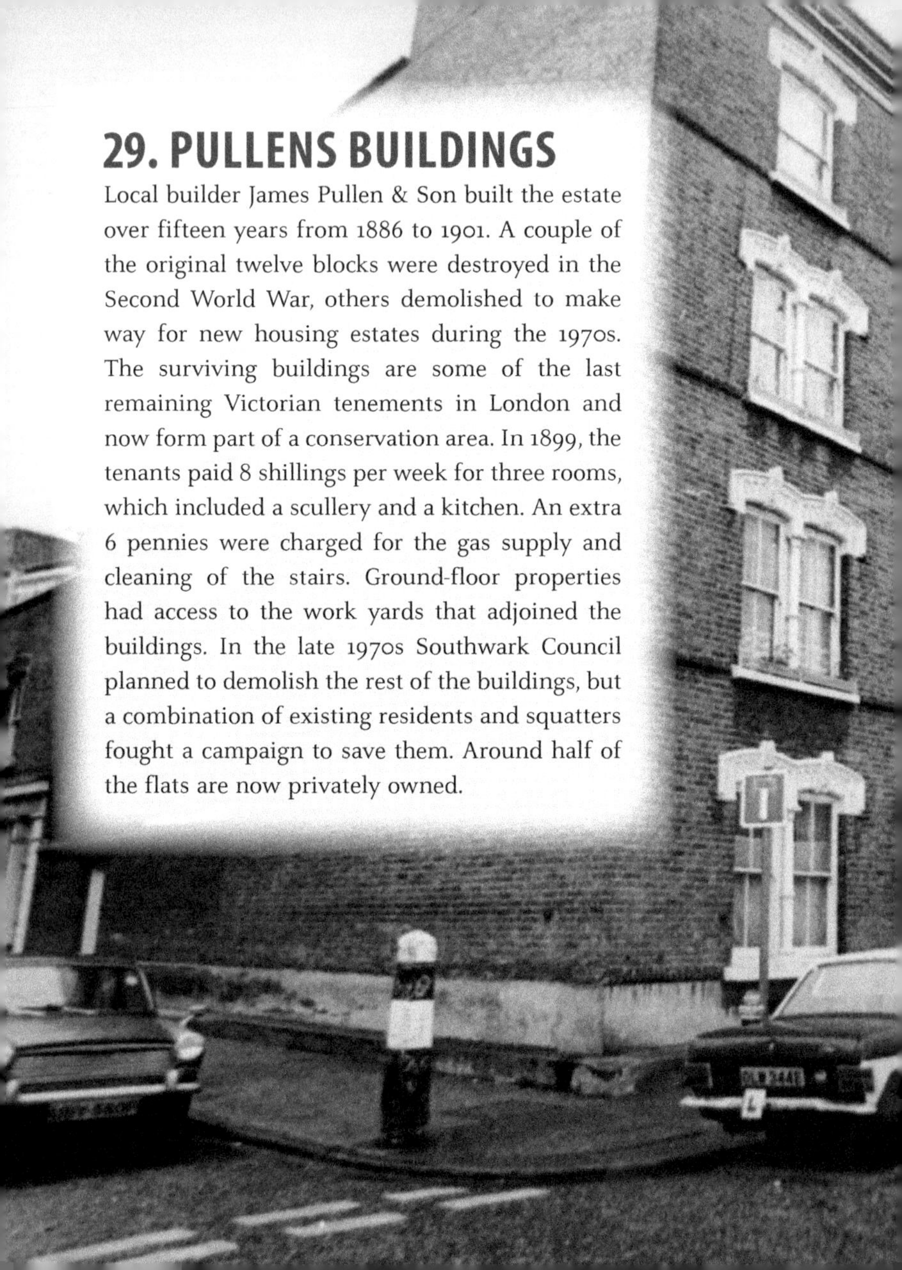

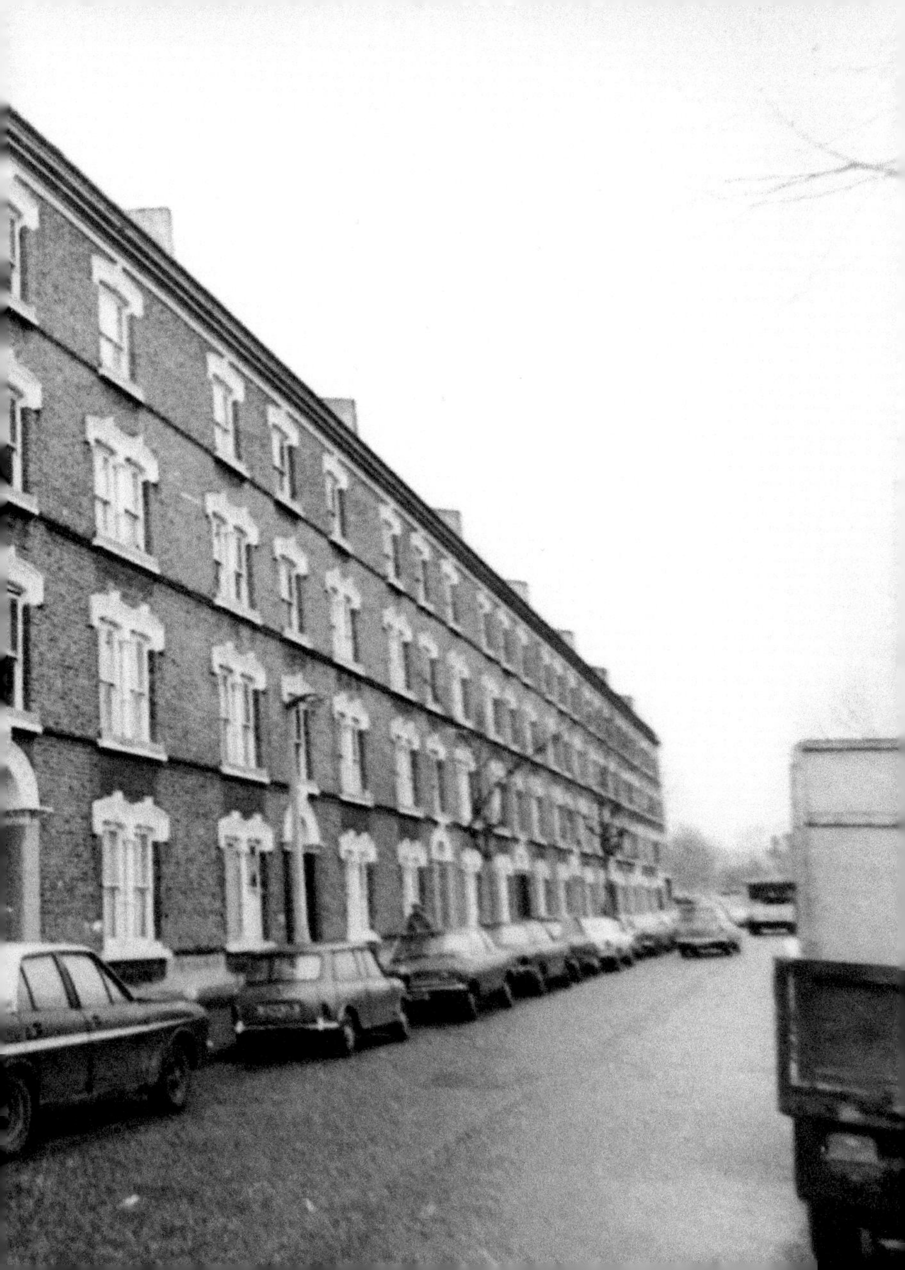

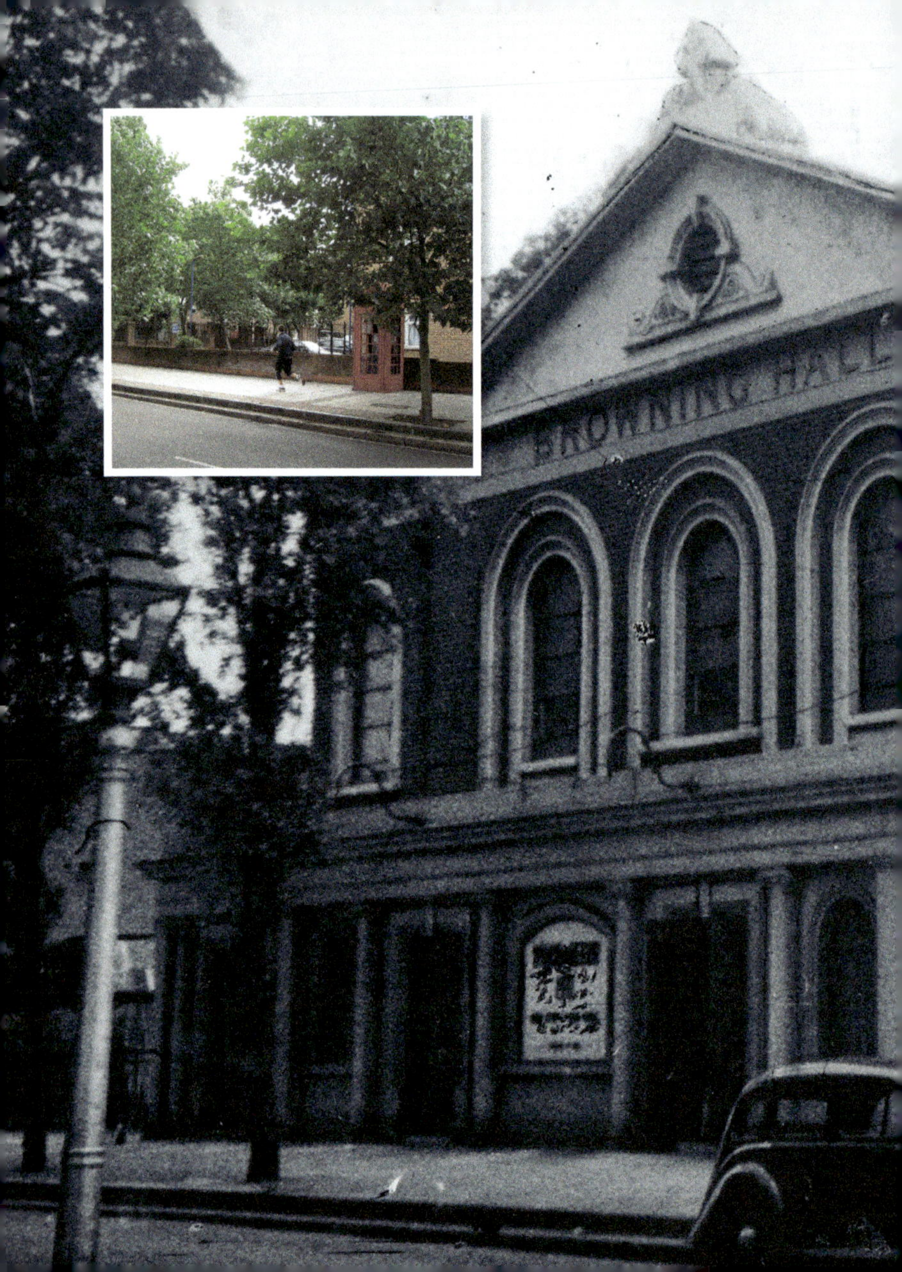
BROWNING HALL

30. BROWNING HALL

Formerly an independent church built in 1790, it was originally known as the York Street Congregational chapel. Robert Browning, one of England's greatest poets, was baptised here in 1812 and the chapel was later renamed after him, as was the street in 1937. During the latter years of the eighteenth century, social work initiated at the chapel did much to ease the suffering of the poor and destitute of Walworth. The Browning Hall was demolished in 1978 after succumbing to fire damage and the Ben Ezra Court housing estate now stands on the site. The telephone box that can be seen in the 1957 photograph is still in situ, and all that remains of the Browning Hall is a tomb dedicated to Richard Holbert and Capt. James Wilson, which can be found on the edge of the housing estate.

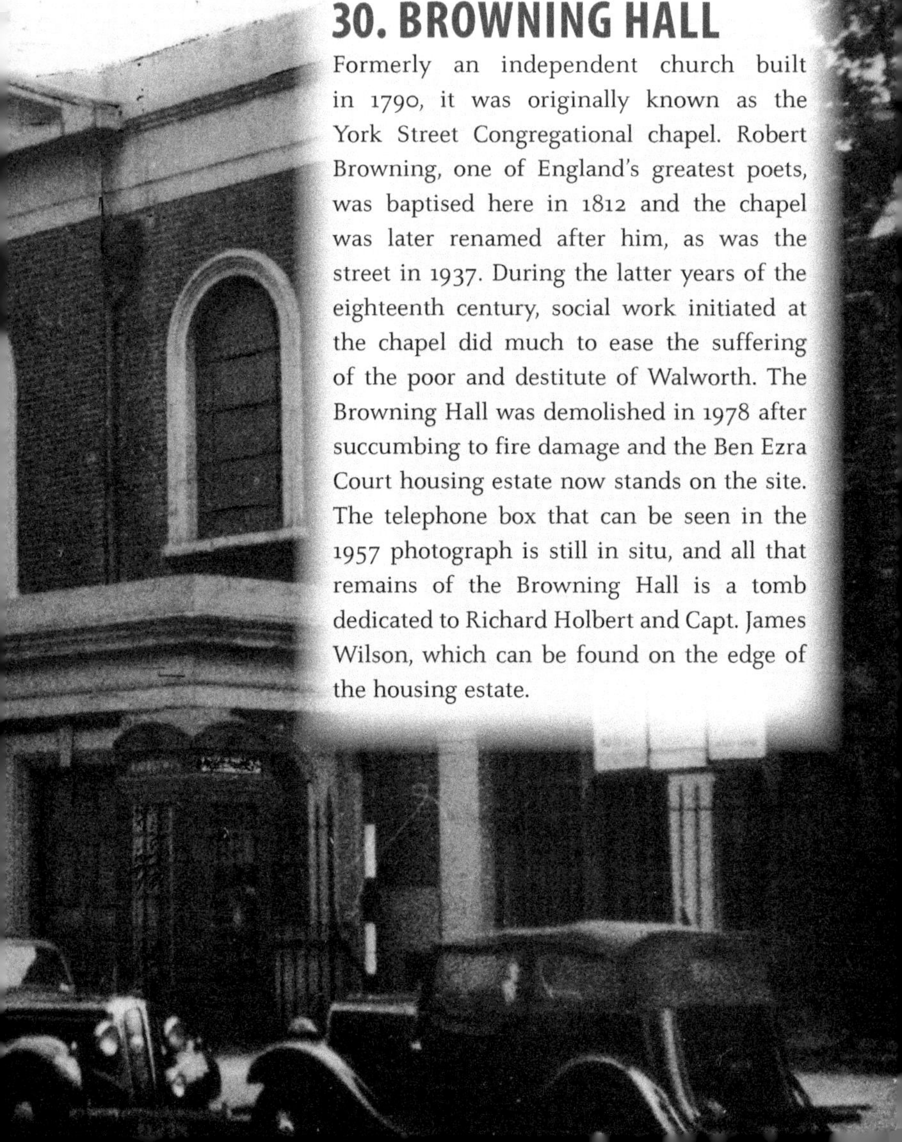

31. HERBERT MORRISON HOUSE

Found on the corner of Browning Street, from 1895 it opened as The Robert Browning Settlement, where medical and legal advice was made available to the poor of SE17. The Settlement was established by Herbert Stead, a social campaigner who later became a key figure in establishing the state funded old aged pension in 1908.

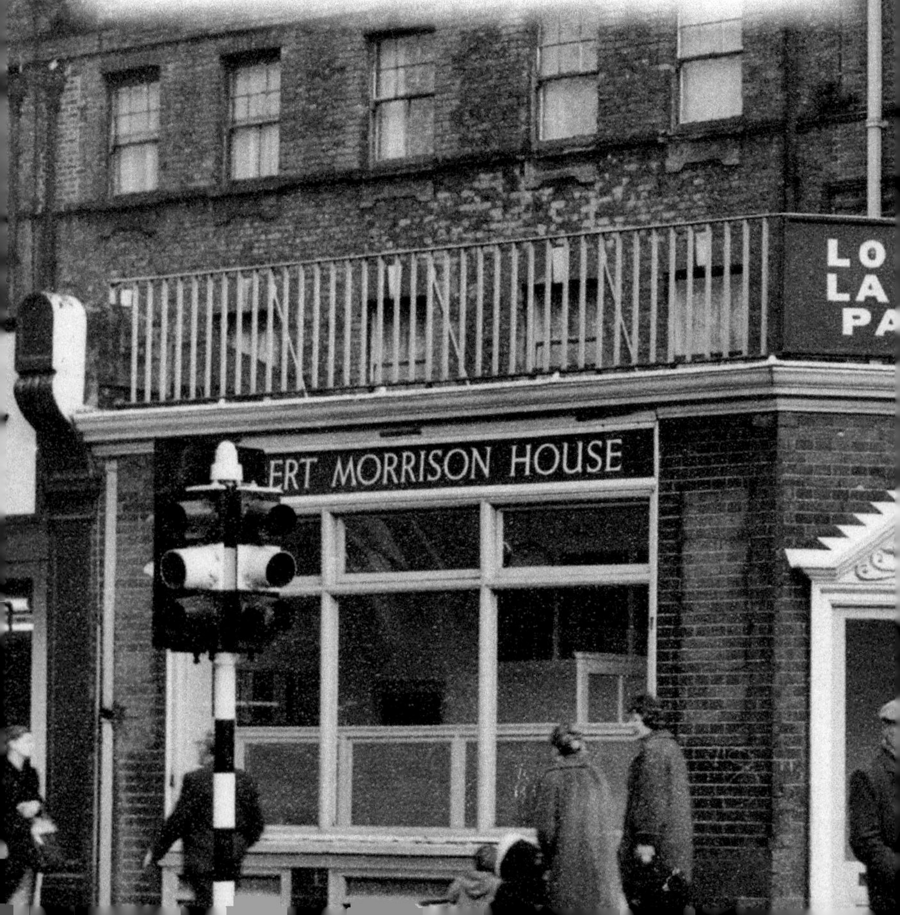

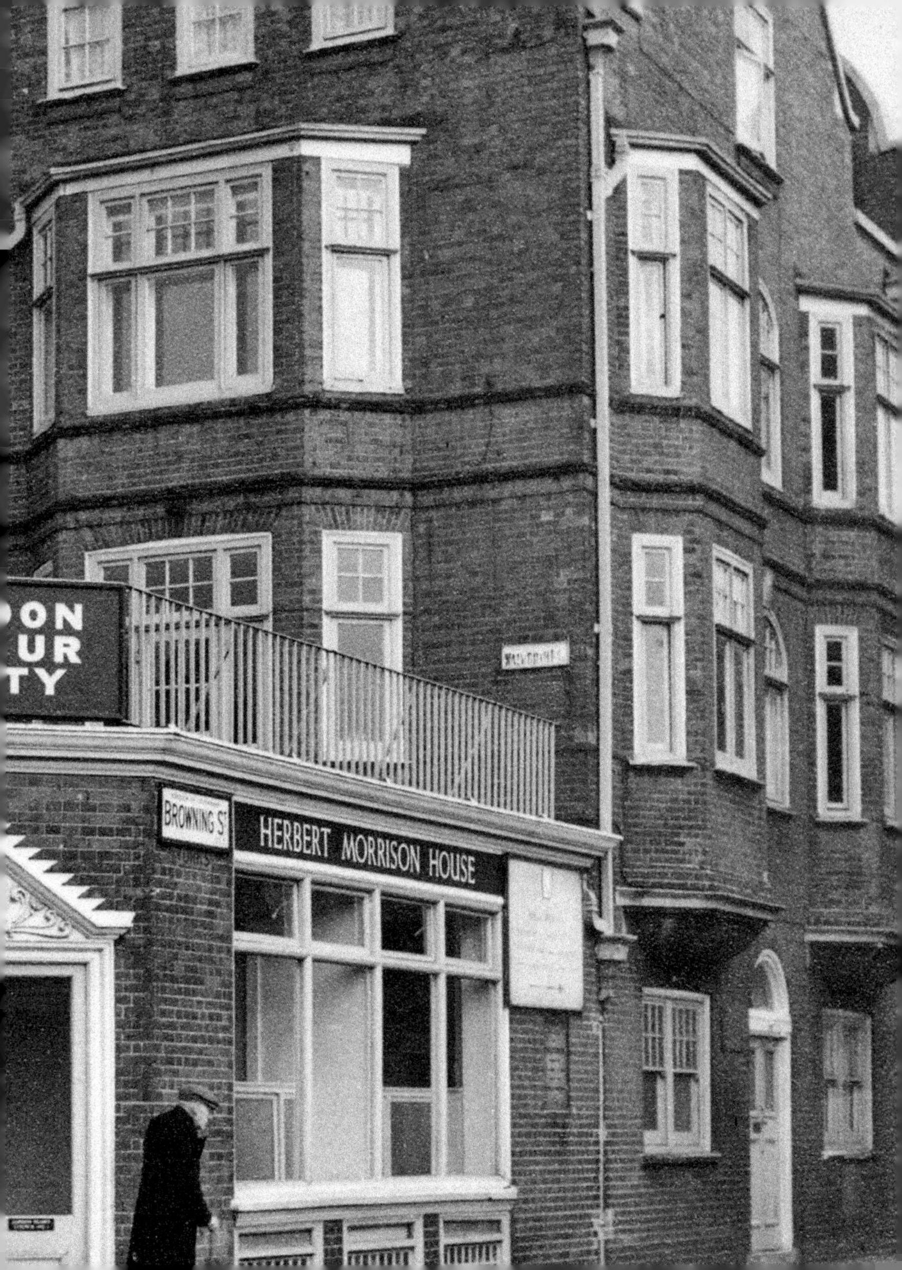
OON
UR
TY
BROWNING ST
HERBERT MORRISON HOUSE

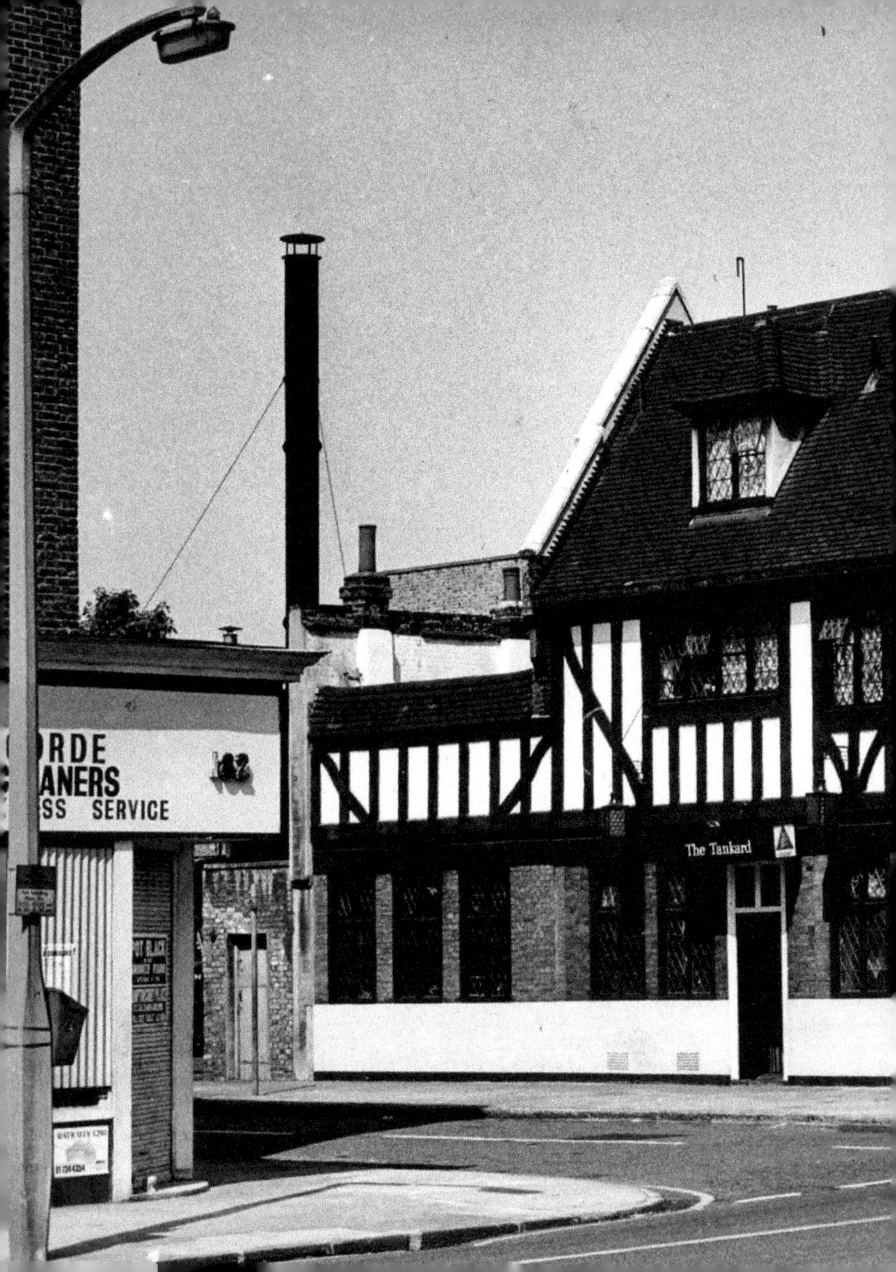
ORDE
ANERS
SS SERVICE
The Tankard

32. THE TANKARD

A mid-nineteenth-century mock-Tudor pub situated at No. 178 Walworth Road on the corner of Amelia Street. A welcoming design with especially beautiful red-brick chimney stacks. The Tankard was well used by many local newly wed couples in years gone by for their wedding receptions, following marriage ceremonies conducted at the old town hall across the road at No. 157.

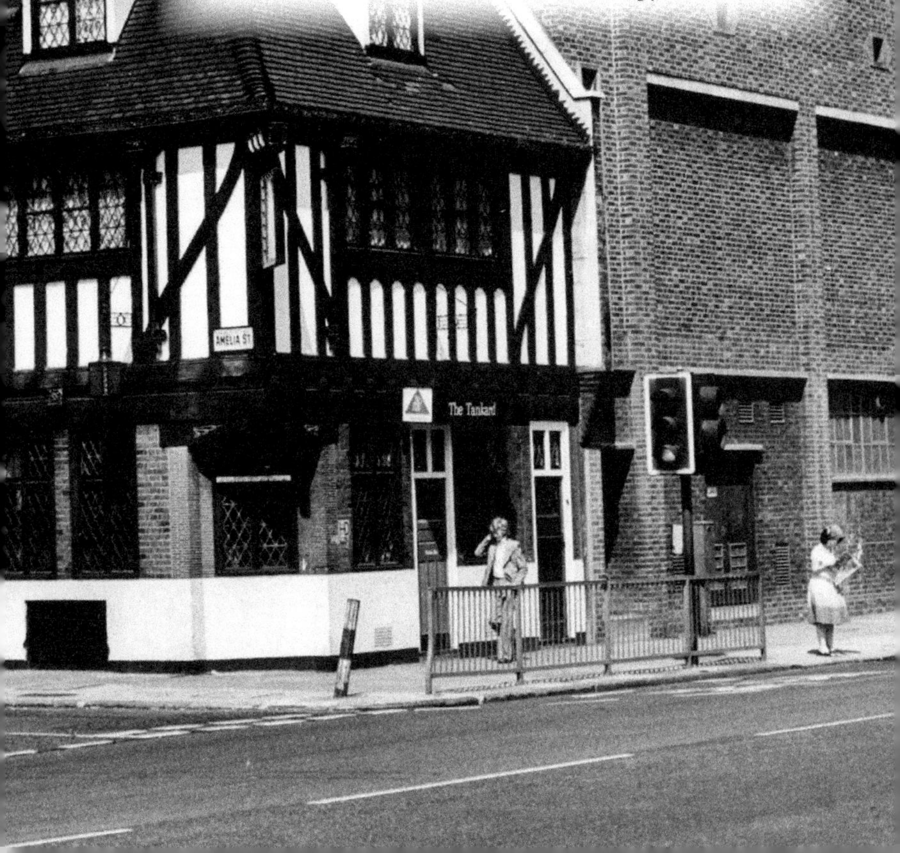

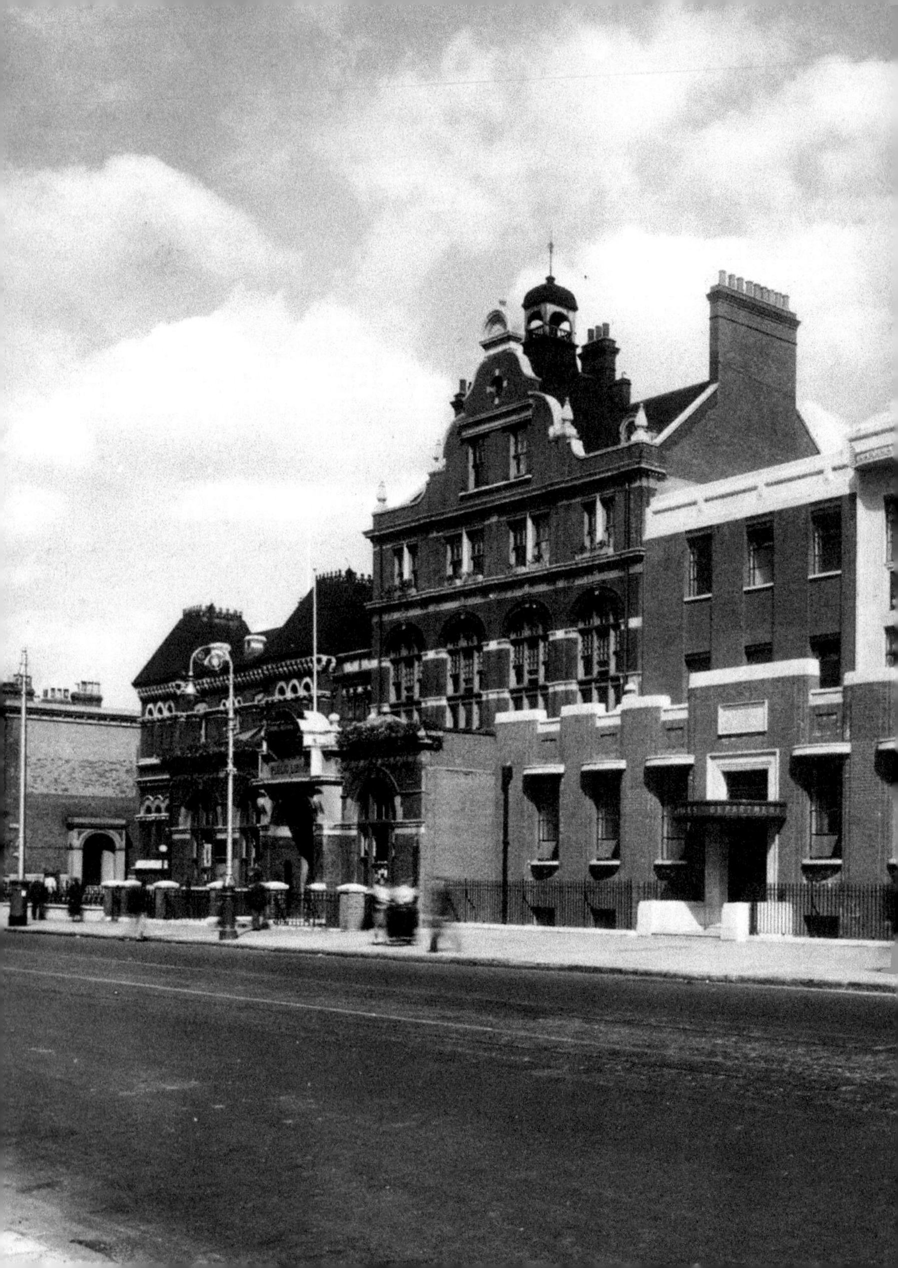

33. THE WALWORTH CLINIC

Formerly known as the Public Health Centre of Southwark, the clinic stands on the corner of the Walworth Road and Larcom Street. Grade II listed, it was designed for the Borough of Southwark by Percy Smart and built between 1936–37. A plaque above the door declares 'The health of the people is the highest law'. This pioneering health centre was well established in advance of the National Health Service Act of 1946. It comprised a solarium, TB clinic, X-ray department, a dentist clinic and a maternity and child welfare centre. Still in use today, the clinic specialises in family planning and offers sexual health advice. Southwark Council blue plaques dedicated to Charles Babbage and Michael Faraday can be seen on the building via Larcom Street.

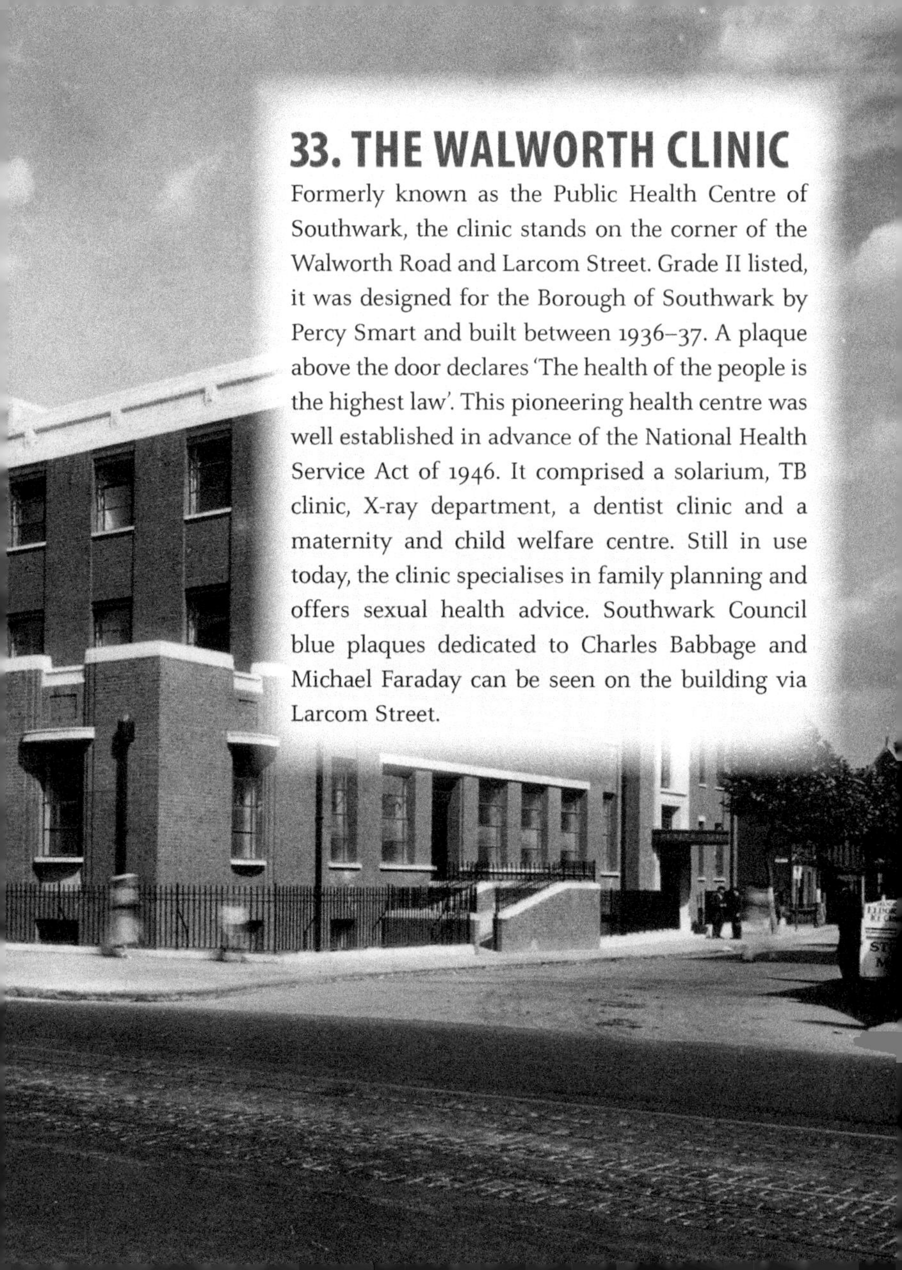

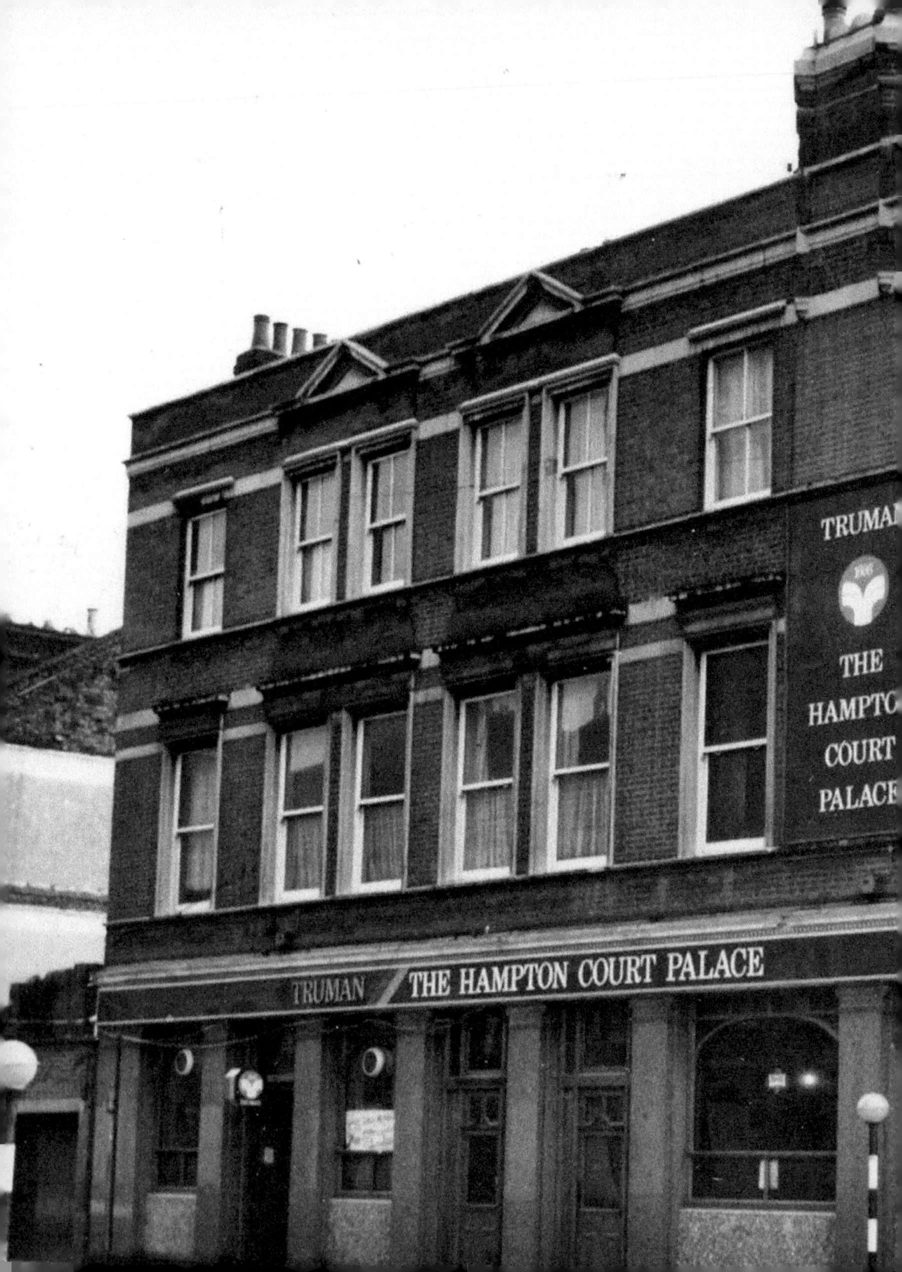
TRUMAN
THE HAMPTON COURT PALACE
TRUMAN
THE HAMPTON COURT PALACE

34. HAMPTON COURT PALACE

This imposing and impressive mid-nineteenth-century pub, with its name stone carved at the highest point of the building, once had a hall that could seat 100 for dinner. Members of the 'Odd Fellows' societies of the day would regularly meet there. Somewhat off the beaten track, it is situated near the Newington Estate, at No. 35 Hampton Street. Over the years, it has had a fine reputation for its food and the live entertainment it provided with a succession of singers and bands performing the hit songs of the day on most nights. The house band went by the name of The Swinging Hamptons.

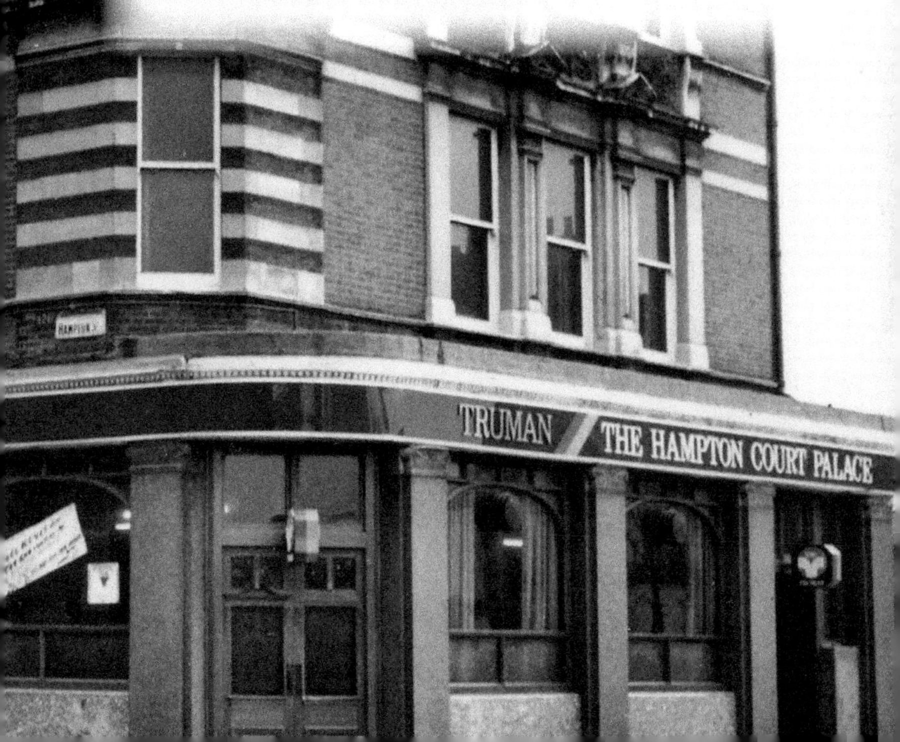

35. RAILWAY BRIDGE

The redevelopment work on the Elephant and Castle in the late 1940s can be seen taking shape under the railway bridge, at the top of the Walworth Road. An advert for the nearby Trocadero Cinema can be seen on the side of the bridge. 'The Troc', which seated 3,500 people, closed in October 1963. Seen behind the bridge in 2010 is Strata SE1, the tallest residential building in central London, which stands at forty-three storeys high and which is part of the new regeneration scheme for the area. Designed by the architects BFLS, building work was completed in 2010 and it comprises 408 high quality apartments with space for shops and restaurants below. One of the interesting design details of the new building are the integrated wind turbines which will generate enough energy to meet the demands of thirty, two-bedroom apartments.

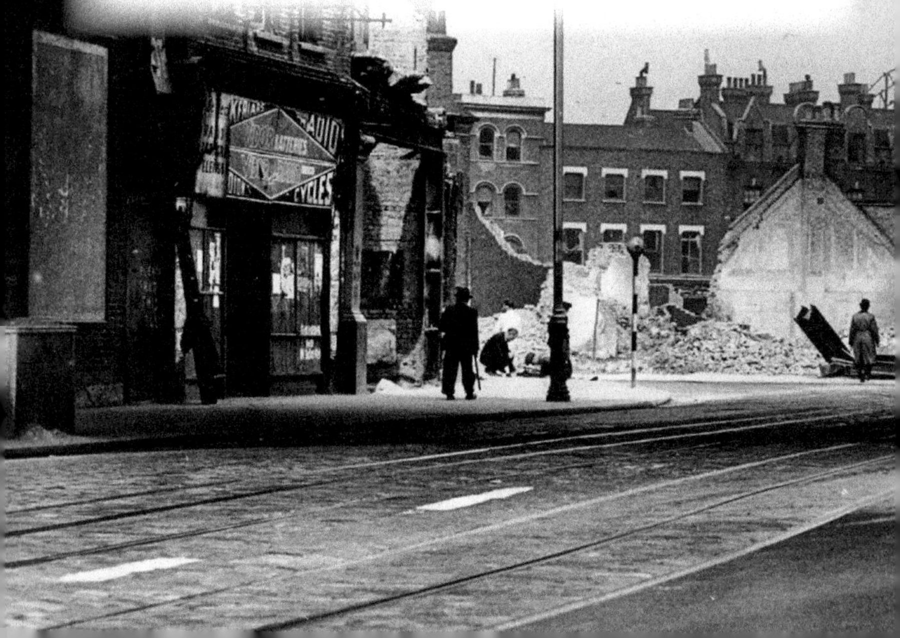

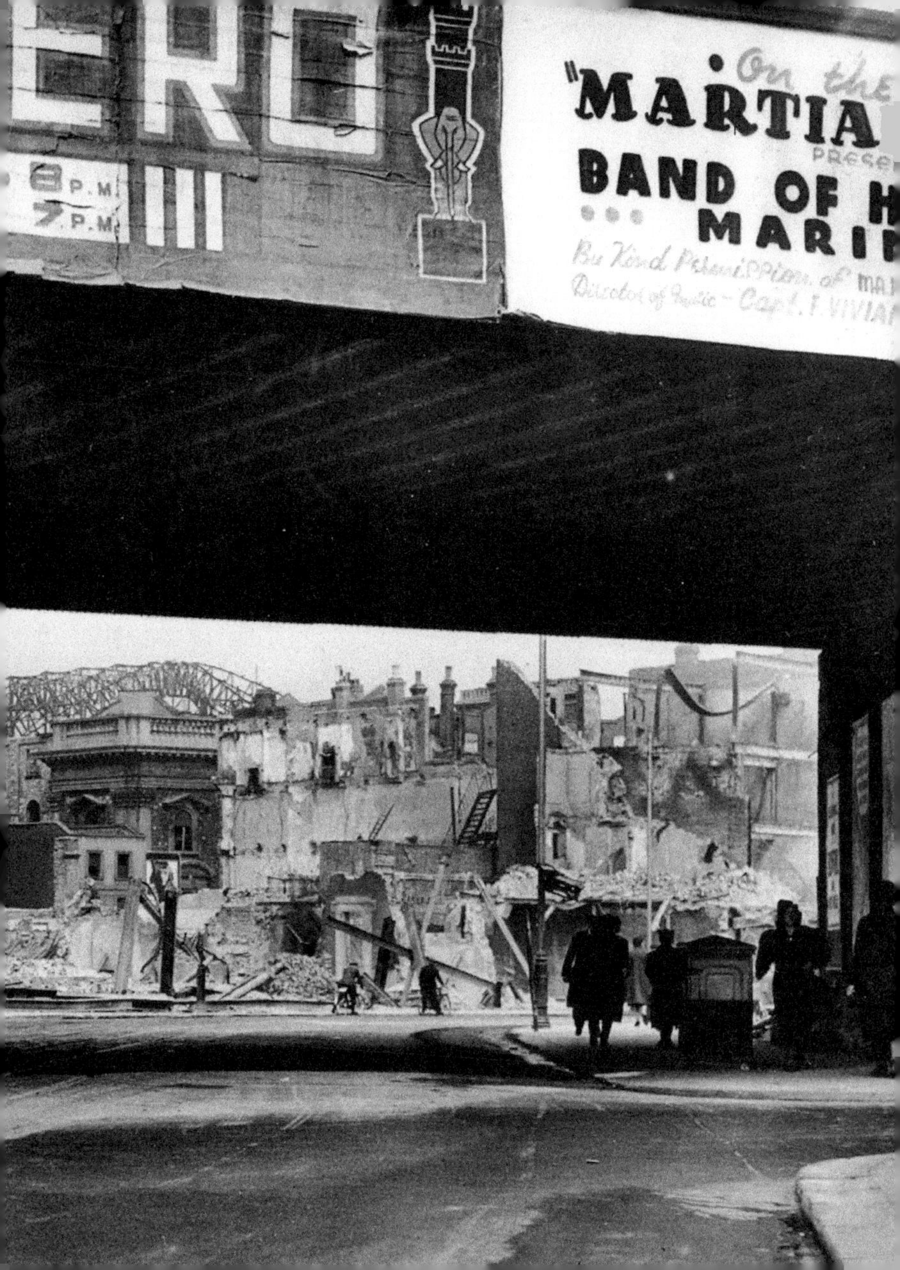
"MARTIA
BAND OF H
MARI
8 P.M
7 P.M

36. TOP OF WALWORTH ROAD

Looking down from the Elephant and Castle, the majority of shops and flats on the left-hand side of the road were demolished to make way for the Heygate Estate development in the late 1960s. Across the road on the right-hand side, the majority of these late nineteenth-century buildings remain intact. The shops there now are mainly food outlets. At Nos 80–82 stands the popular The Ivory Arch Indian restaurant. The Electric Picture Palace cinema, opened in 1910 at No. 88, and is now flats. Further left, the light blue paintwork identifies Julian Markham House at No. 114. This provides accommodation for those studying at the various local art colleges. The Dragon Castle Chinese restaurant forms the lower part of this building.

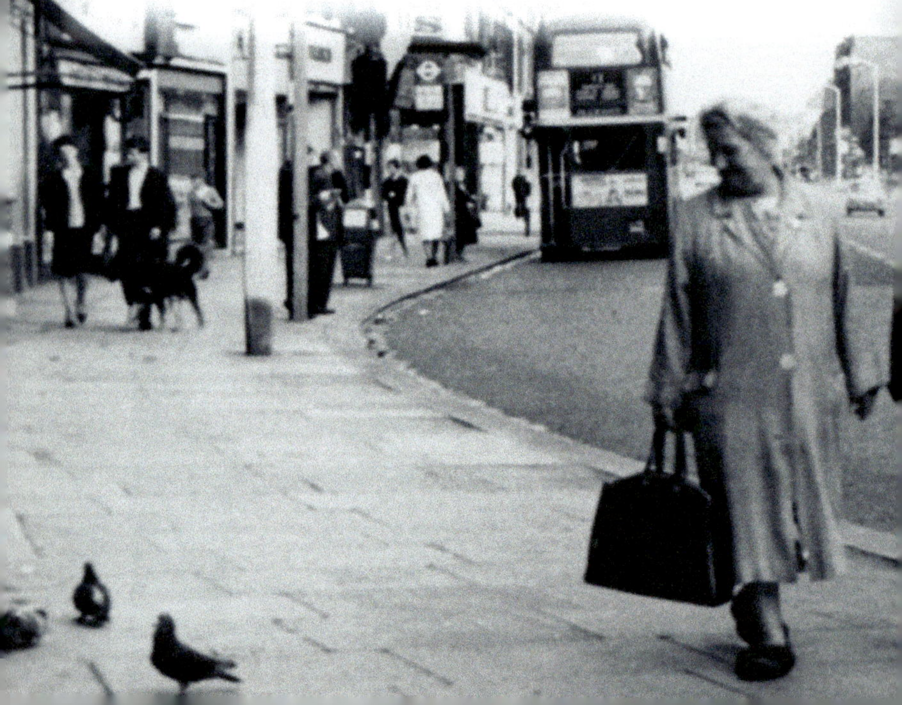

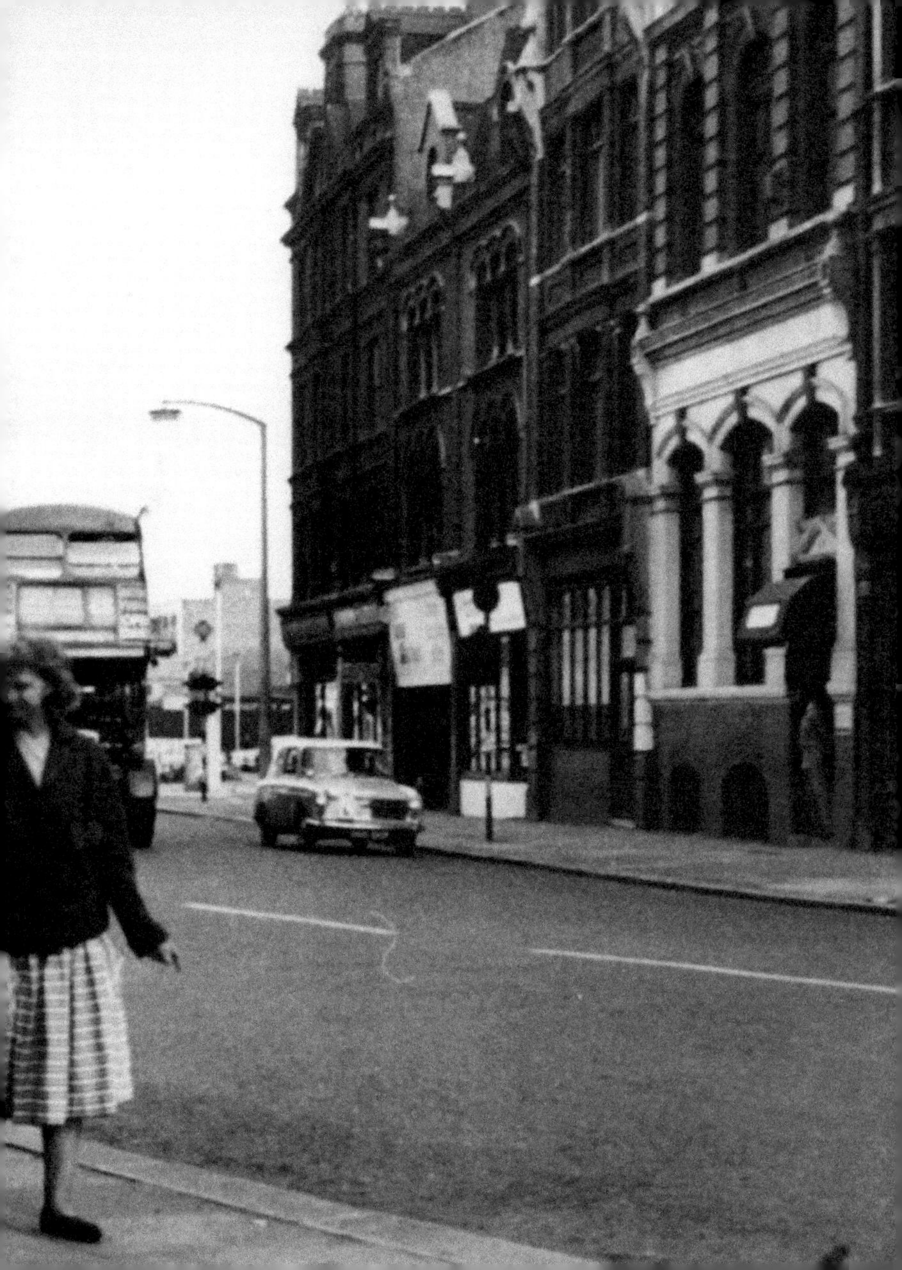

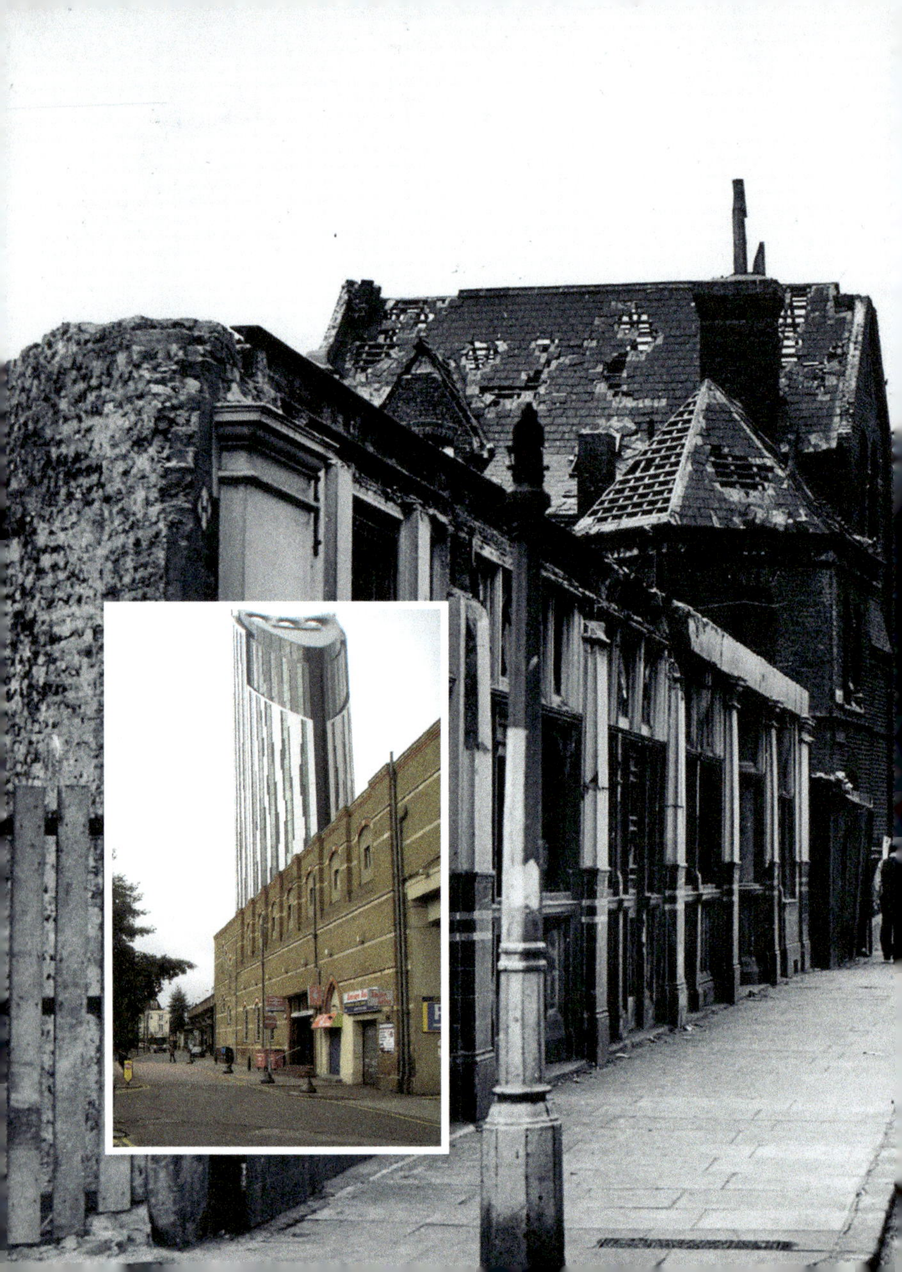

37. ELEPHANT ROAD

Looking towards Walworth Road directly behind the Elephant and Castle Shopping Centre, the buildings on the left have all been demolished and that area now forms Elephant Road Park. An entrance to the Elephant and Castle railway station is situated to the right. The station, built on a brick viaduct, opened in 1862. Various small businesses trade from within the 22 foot high and 25 foot wide railway arches. Among them is the Corsica Studios, an independent arts space and venue; the Re-Cycling second-hand bike shop; and a couple of South American cafés. Each year the Carnival de Pueblo, Europe's biggest Latin American street carnival begins its journey to nearby Burgess Park from here.

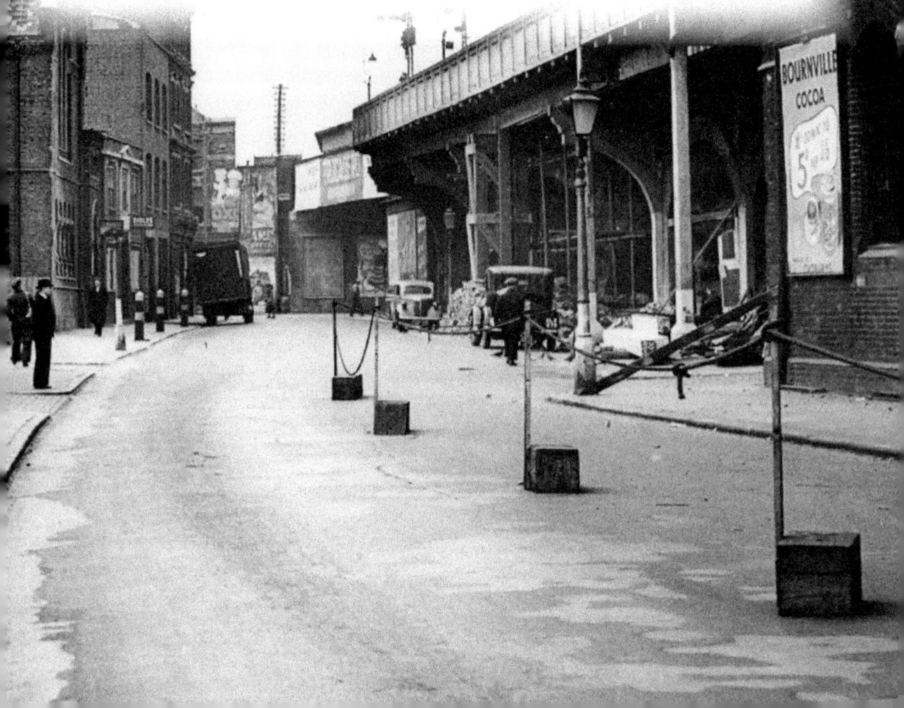

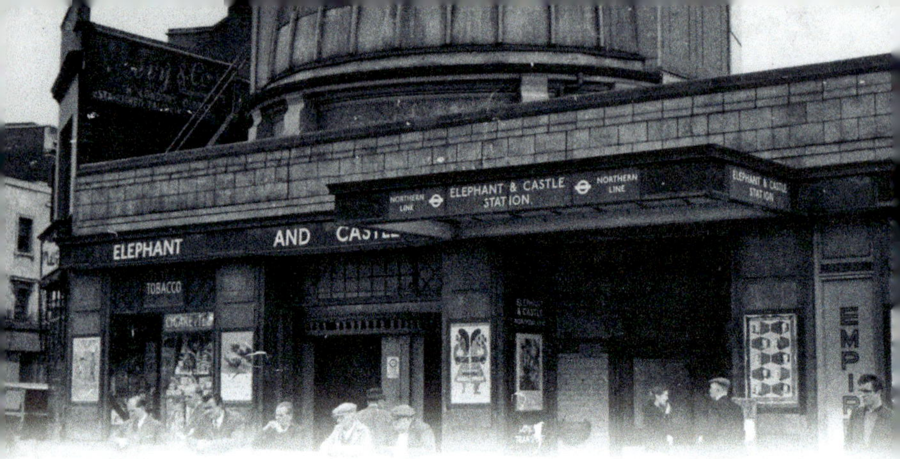

38. ELEPHANT & CASTLE TUBE STATION

Designed by Thomas Phillips Figgis and built in 1890, the station has been modernised and rebuilt over the years, with its final incarnation unveiled in 2003. It services both the Bakerloo and Northern tube lines. The first baby born on the underground system was born at this station in 1924. Reports at the time claiming she was named Thelma Ursula Beatrice Eleanor, thus spelling TUBE, were later proven to be false, with her real name being Maria Cordery.

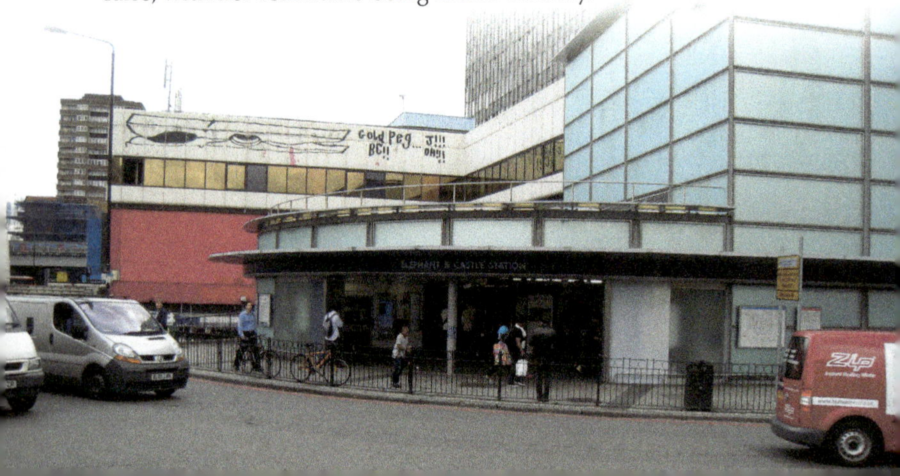

39. HEYGATE ESTATE

Vast swathes of SE17 were demolished to make way for the building of the Heygate Estate, which was completed in 1974. The 'Brutalist' style housing blocks were built and assembled on site from pre-fabricated concrete. A total of 1,194 modern homes were provided, many for those who had moved from the traditional 'two up, two down' terraced housing. However, design faults soon became apparent with crime and vandalism relatively easy to commit on the estate, but proving difficult to prevent.

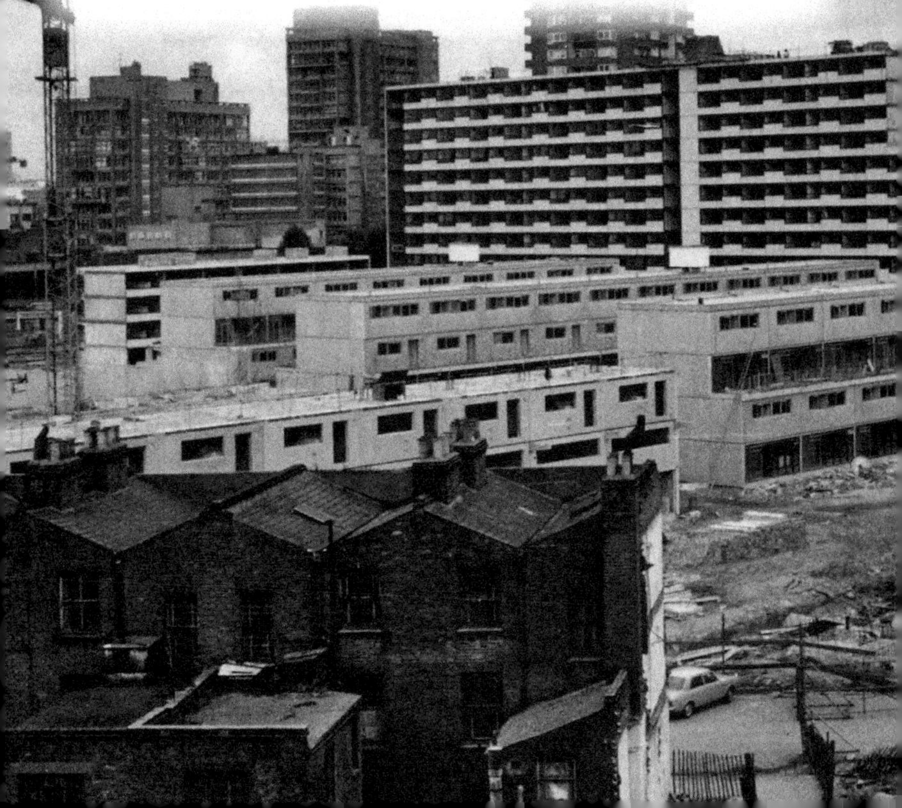

40. WALTERS CLOSE

John Walters, a clerk to the Drapers' Company (1616–56), founded almshouses in Southwark in the 1650s and Walters Close was founded as a part of that project. Over the years it has moved to various locations in the borough, finally settling in Brandon Street in 1961. Walters Close, with its clock tower and courtyards, is divided into forty-three sheltered housing flats, comprising a mixture of bedsits and one- and two-bedroom accommodation all in beautifully maintained surroundings.

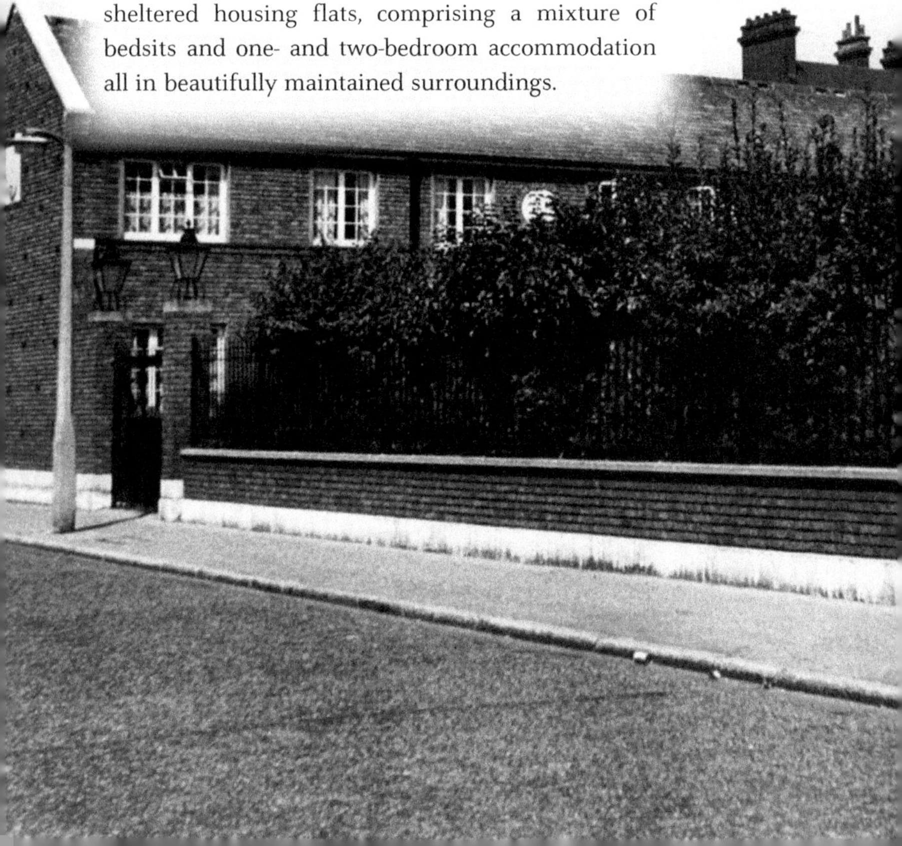

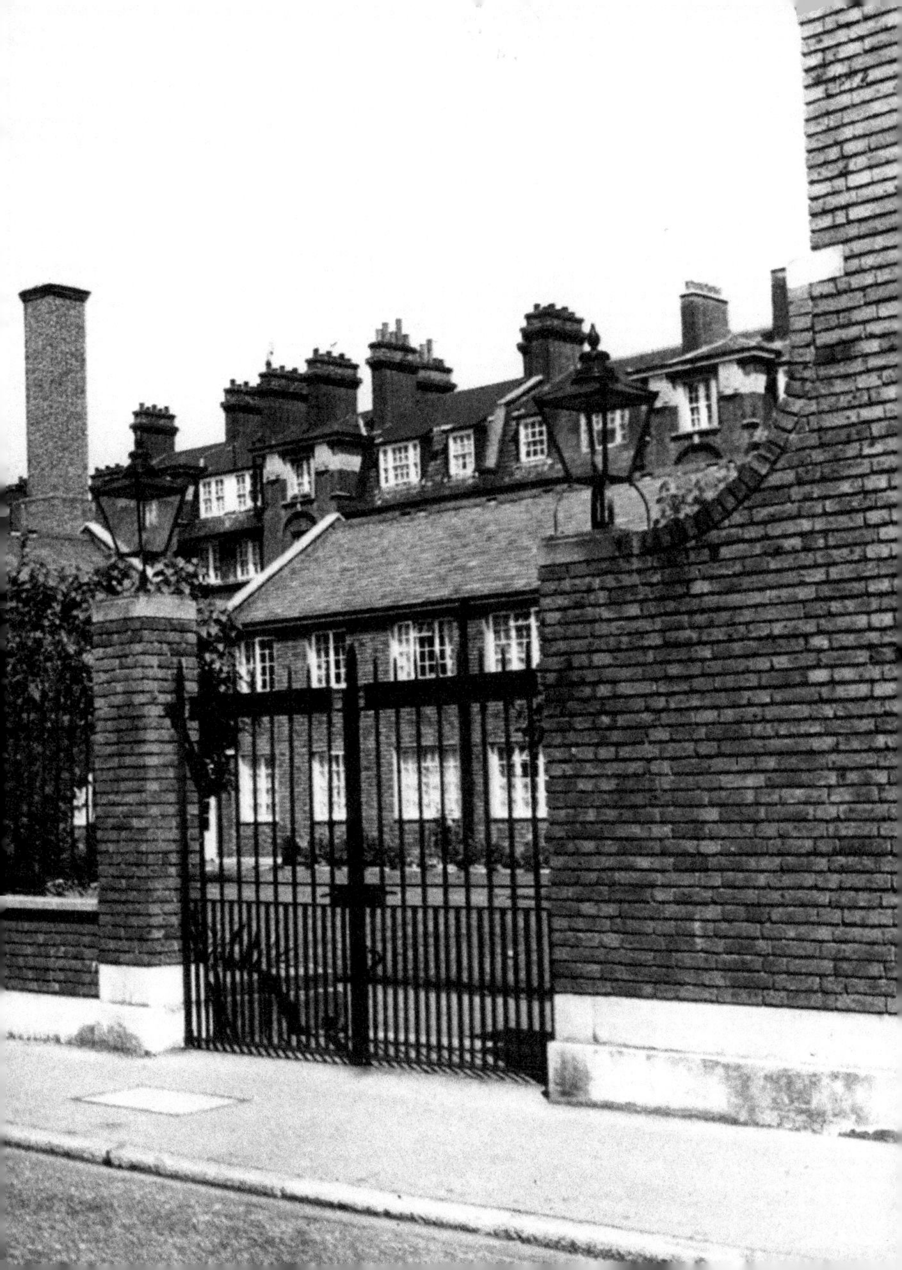

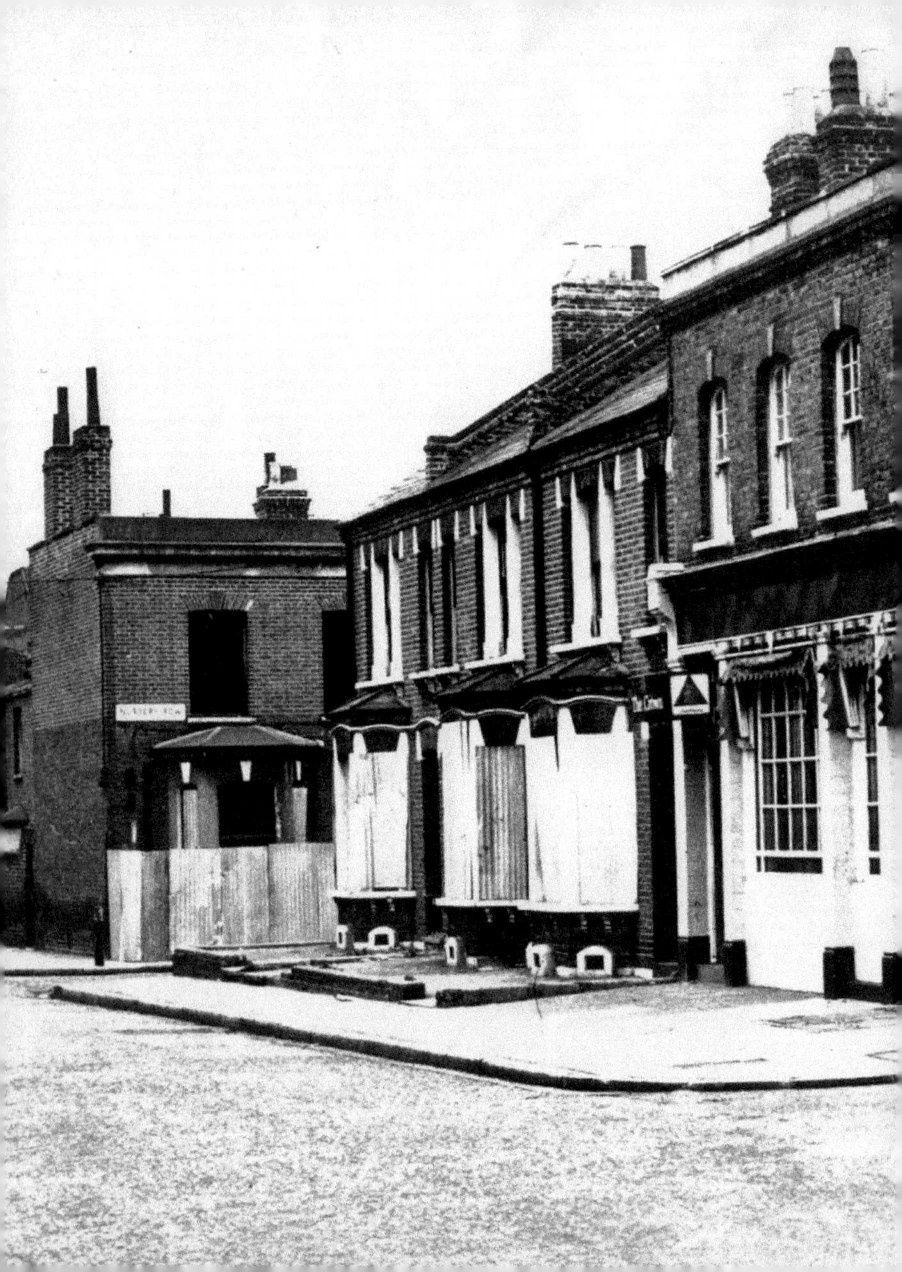

The Crown

41. BRANDON STREET

The Crown pub is still standing while all around it has changed dramatically in this turning off of Browning Street. The original glazed earthenware 'faience' tiling on the pub has made it very popular with film and television crews. It appeared in an episode of the BBC drama *Ashes to Ashes*.

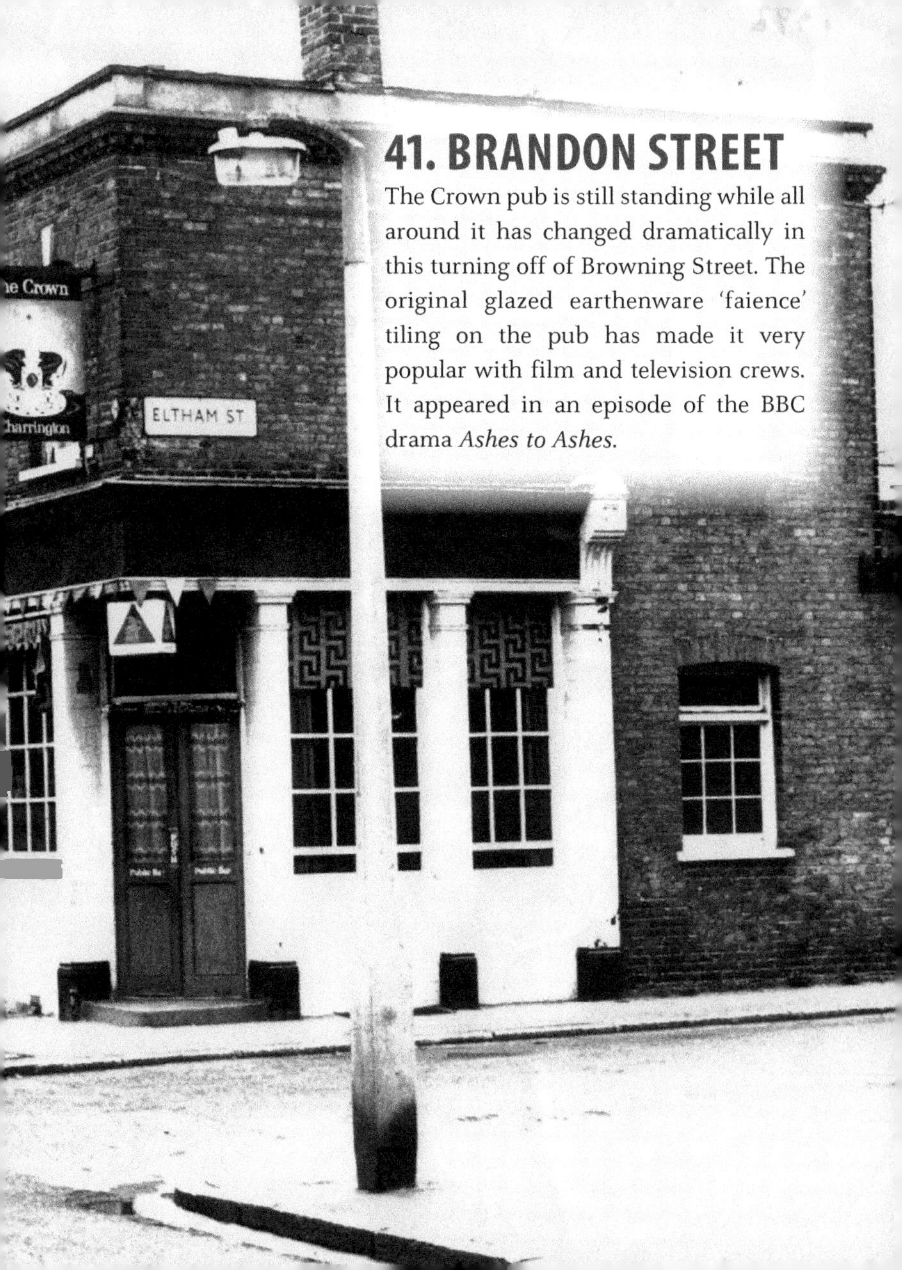

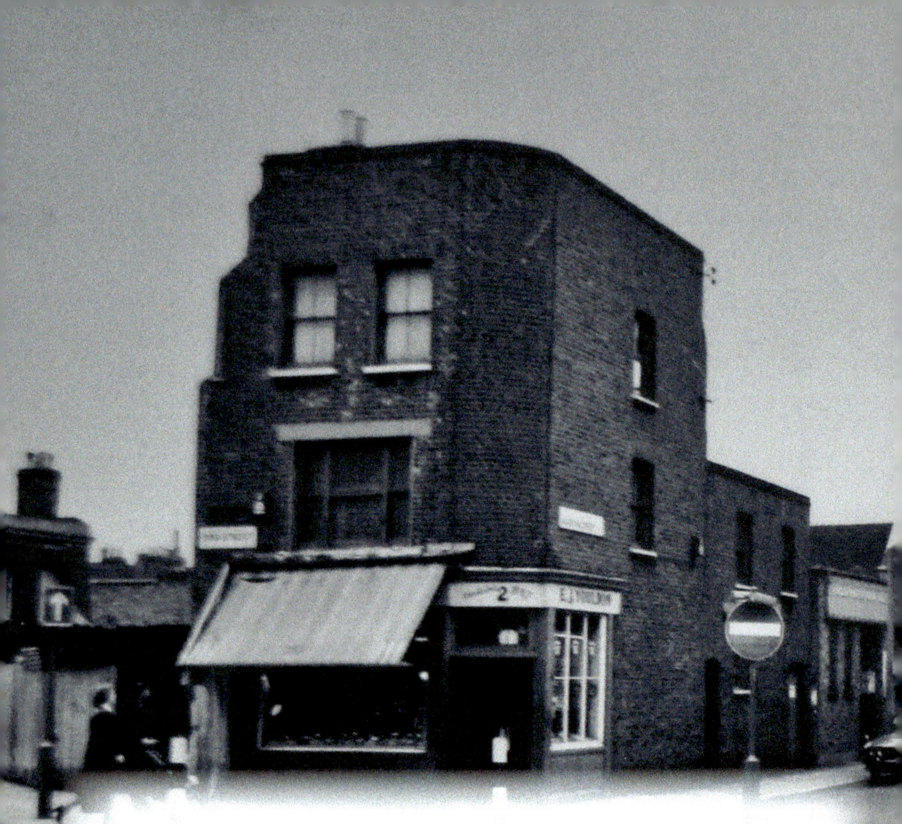

42. RODNEY ROAD

Named after a son of the local property developer Edward Yates, this stretch has a few interesting buildings. The Rose & Crown is a locals' pub situated away in the back streets and stands directly next to a group of Peabody Trust buildings. George Peabody was a wealthy American philanthropist who started his housing trust in 1862 to provide good quality accommodation for the poor of London. The Peabody Group owns and manages 19,000 homes in the capital. To the left of the pub, the butcher's shop has since been demolished.

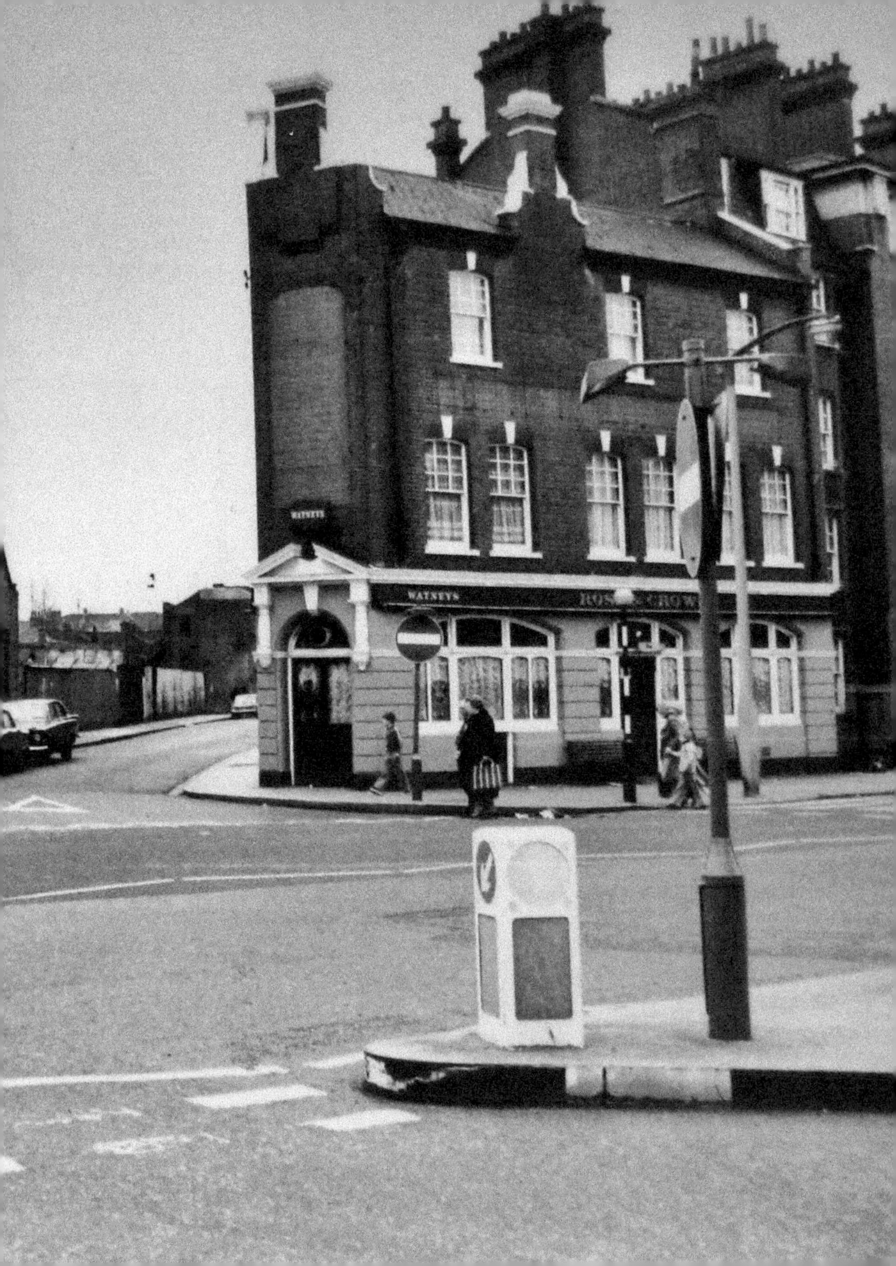
WATNEYS
WATNEYS

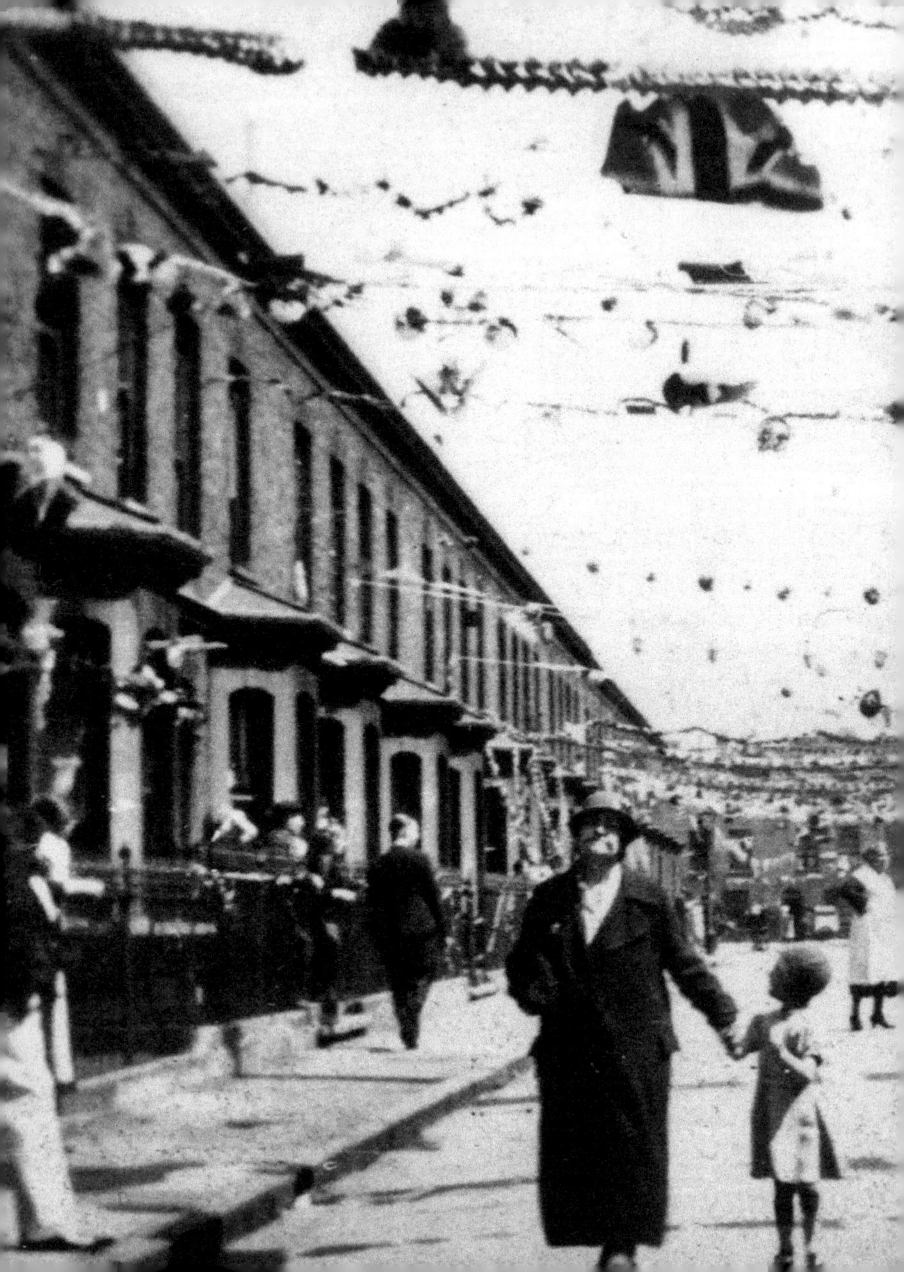

43. NURSERY ROW

A child walking with her grandmother in Nursery Row takes a look at the houses bedecked with union jack flags and bunting on the occasion of the Coronation of King George VI in 1937. So named due to the proliferation of plant nurseries once established here, one side of the Row was owned by the Rolls Estate and the other by the Yates Estate. Edward Yates, the founder, built large areas of housing in Walworth in the late 1880s. The family-run company still have an office at 205 Walworth Road. The flags were put out again on the streets of Walworth in celebration of England taking part in the 2010 World Cup.

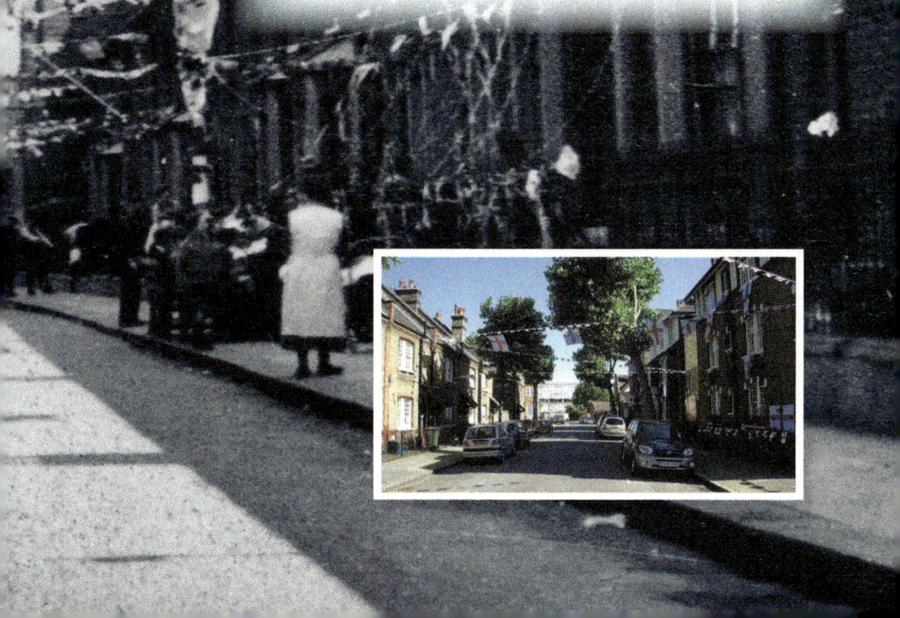

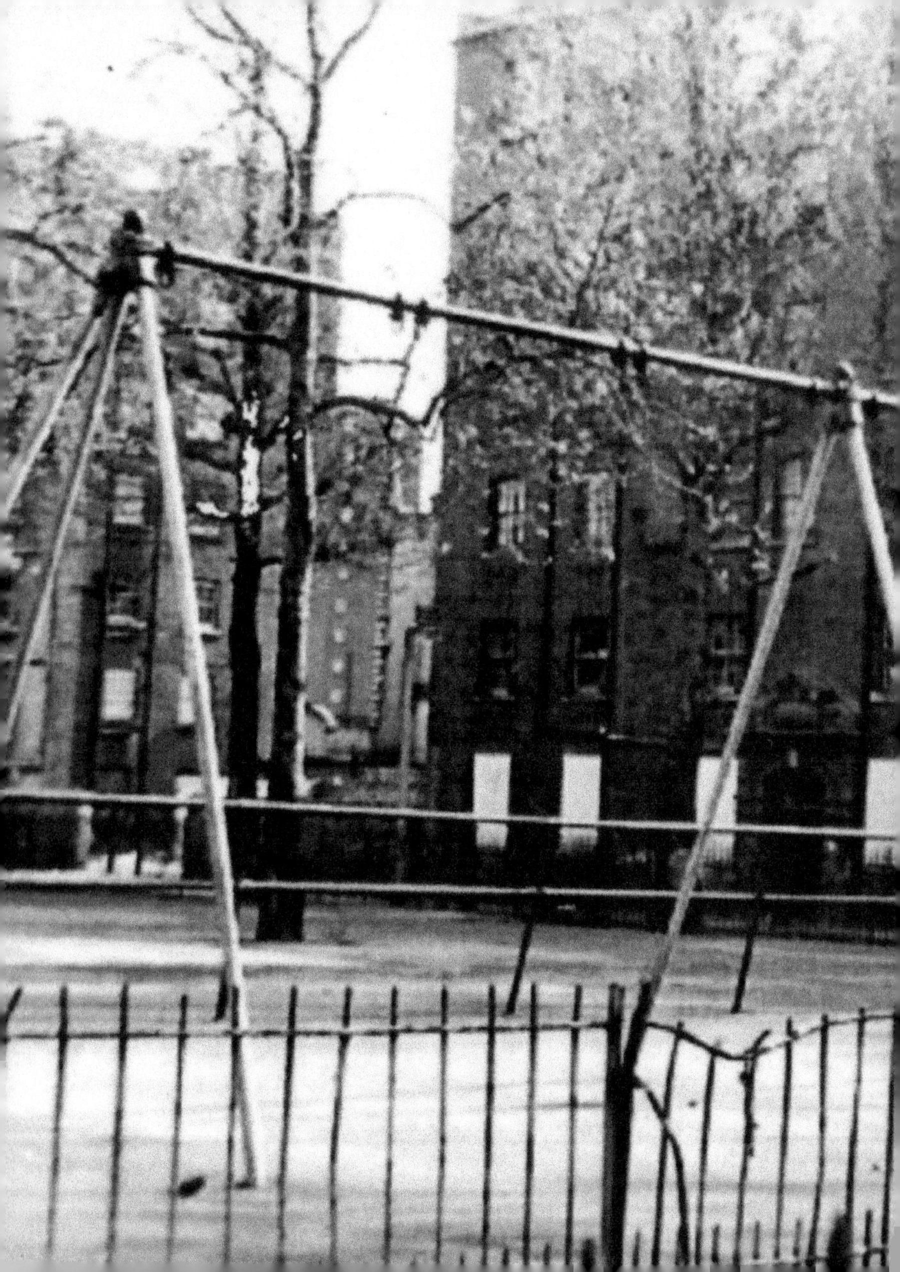

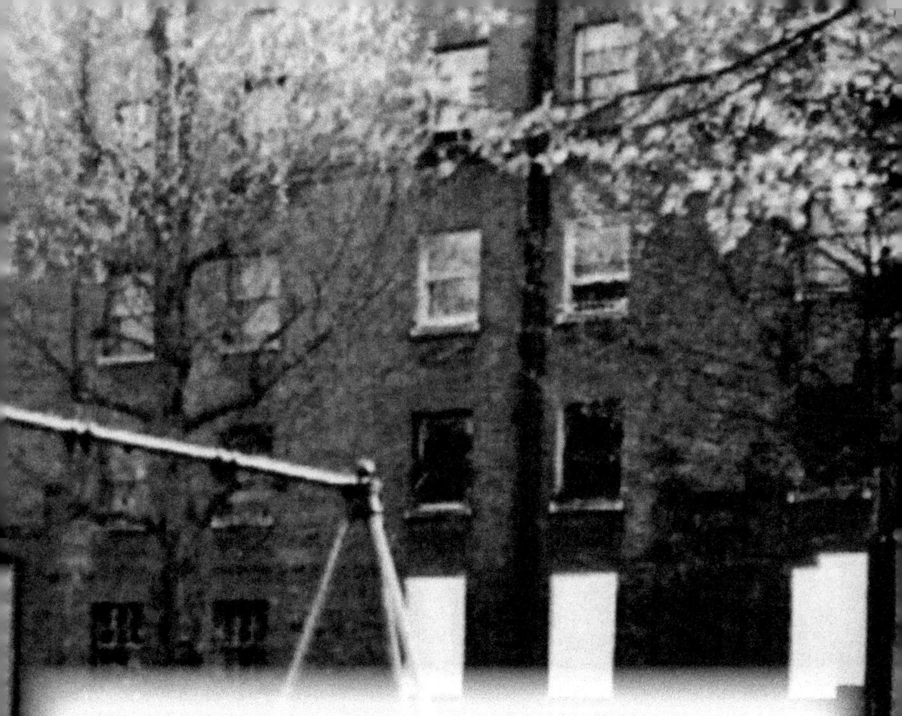

44. BLENDON ROW

These tenement block-style buildings, situated very close to East Street, gained national notoriety when they were featured in the celebrated and award winning 1971 Thames Television documentary *We Was All One* made by the film maker Ken Ashton. The film focused on the way of life lived by those in and around the Elephant and Castle and Bermondsey. The residential blocks were shown to be in a very poor state of repair and overrun with rats. Southwark Council had begun a programme of slum clearance in Walworth as far back as the 1930s, but these blocks were still inhabited for many years after that, with at least three families sharing one toilet. They were eventually demolished in the late 1970s. The area on which they once stood is now a park.

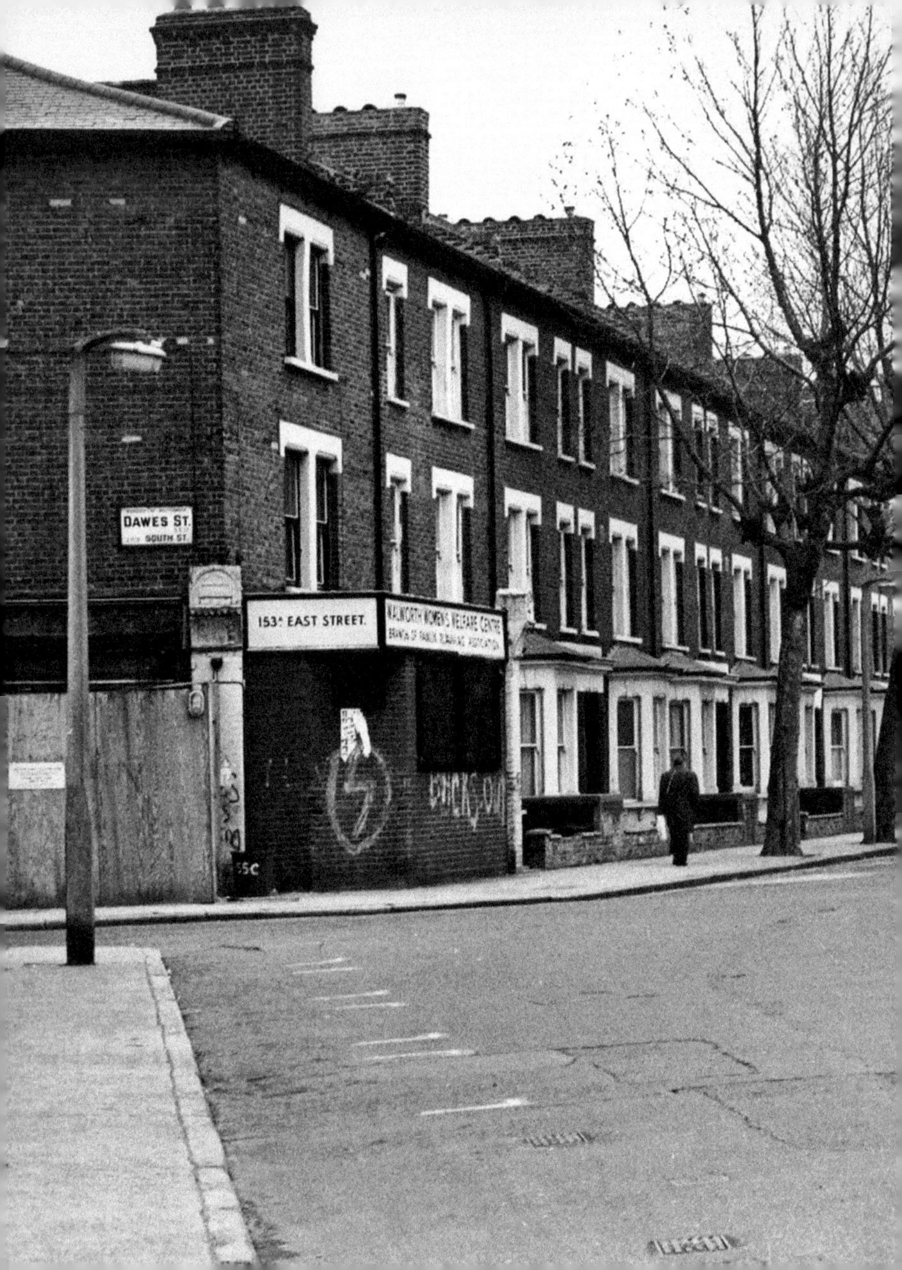
DAWES ST.
SOUTH ST.
153A EAST STREET.
WALWORTH WOMEN'S WELFARE CENTRE
BRANCH OF FAMILY PLANNING ASSOCIATION

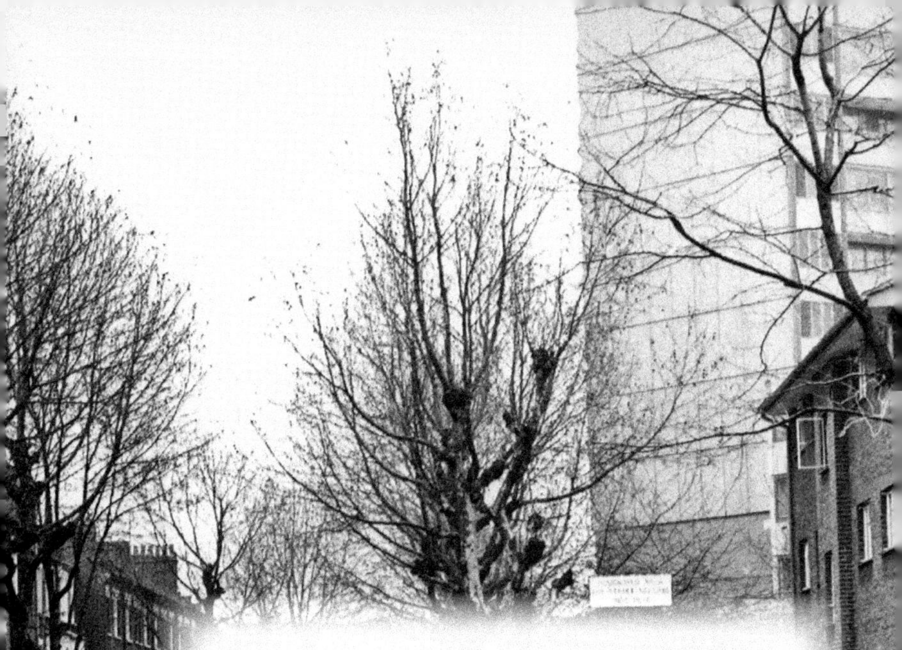

45. CHARLES VICKERY DRYSDALE

Situated at No. 153a East Street on the corner of Dawes Street is a very tatty looking building today. What singles it out for attention is the English Heritage blue plaque upon its wall. In 1921, Doctor Charles Vickery Drysdale opened his first birth control clinic here. The clinic, and the advice it gave, was seen as an enormous help to the local women of Walworth and surrounding areas, many of whom already had large families and were living in terrible conditions on very low wages. Doctor Drysdale later became a founder of the Family Planning Association in 1930. The building, which later became a Brook Clinic dispensing sexual health advice to the under twenty-fives of the area, currently stands empty.

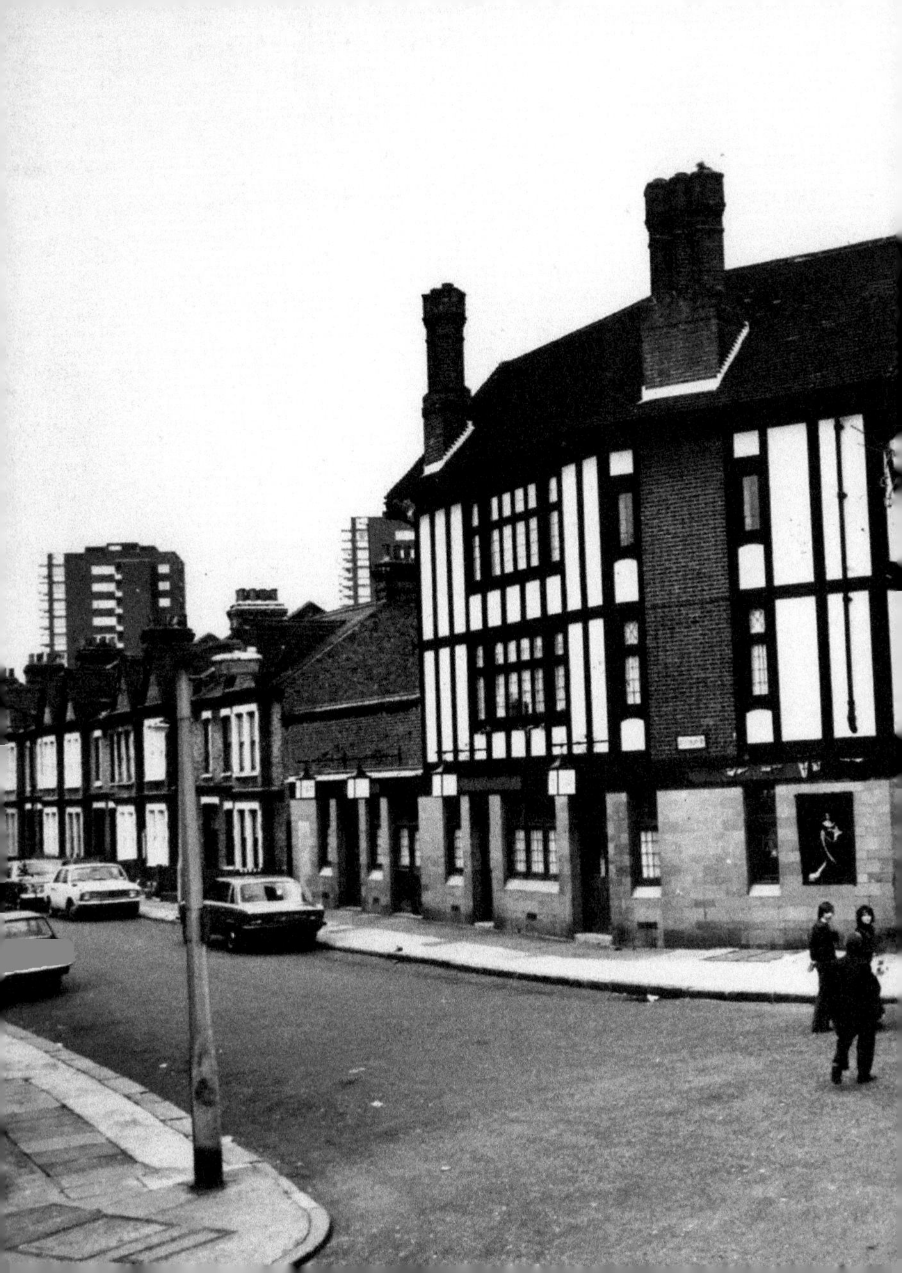

46. THE QUEEN ANNE

A fine example of a mock Tudor style public house, the 'Annie', was situated at No. 126 Dawes Street on the fringes of the Aylesbury Estate. However, it has been converted to flats in the last few years and is now called Old Queen Anne House. In 2008, over 1,900 pubs in the UK closed for good, and this trend is continuing at an alarming rate.

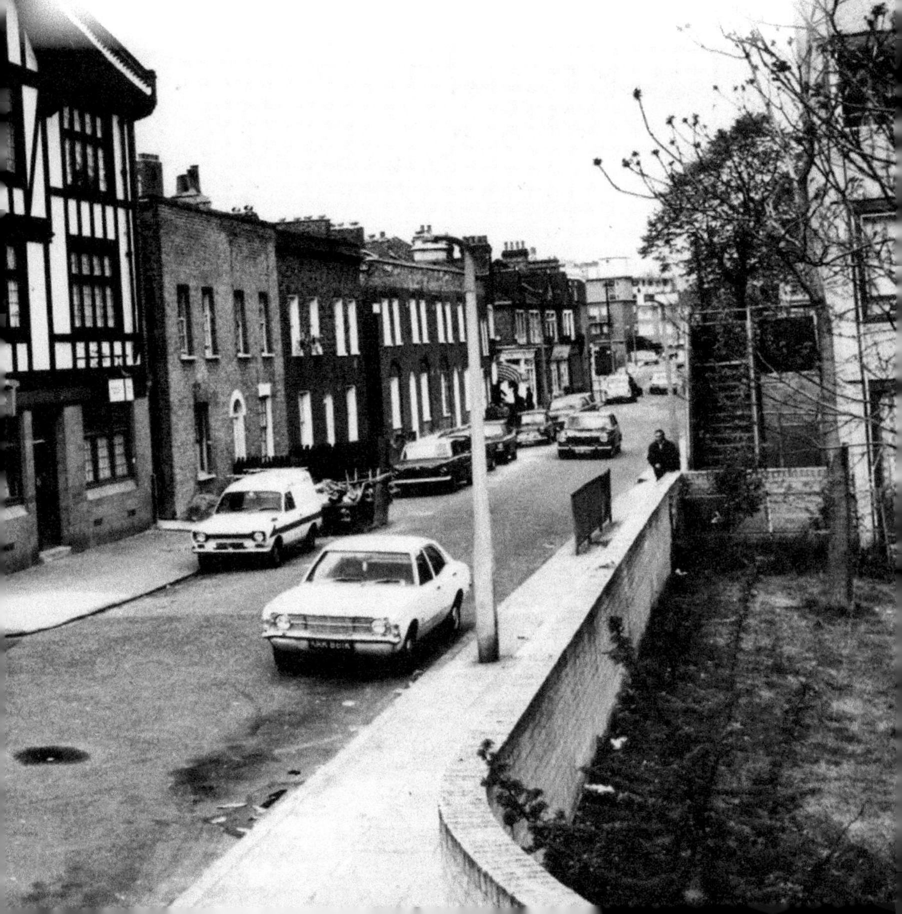

47. SURREY SQUARE

A fine selection of Georgian terraced houses designed by surveyor Michael Searles and built between 1795 and 1796, eighteen of which have survived. The buildings today still have their original torch snuffers and railings and the 'four-kerb' pavement is also an interesting feature. The fan motif pediment in coade stone above the end pavilion is another original surviving detail. Samuel Palmer, the well-known landscape artist, was born at No. 42 (formerly No. 13) in 1805.

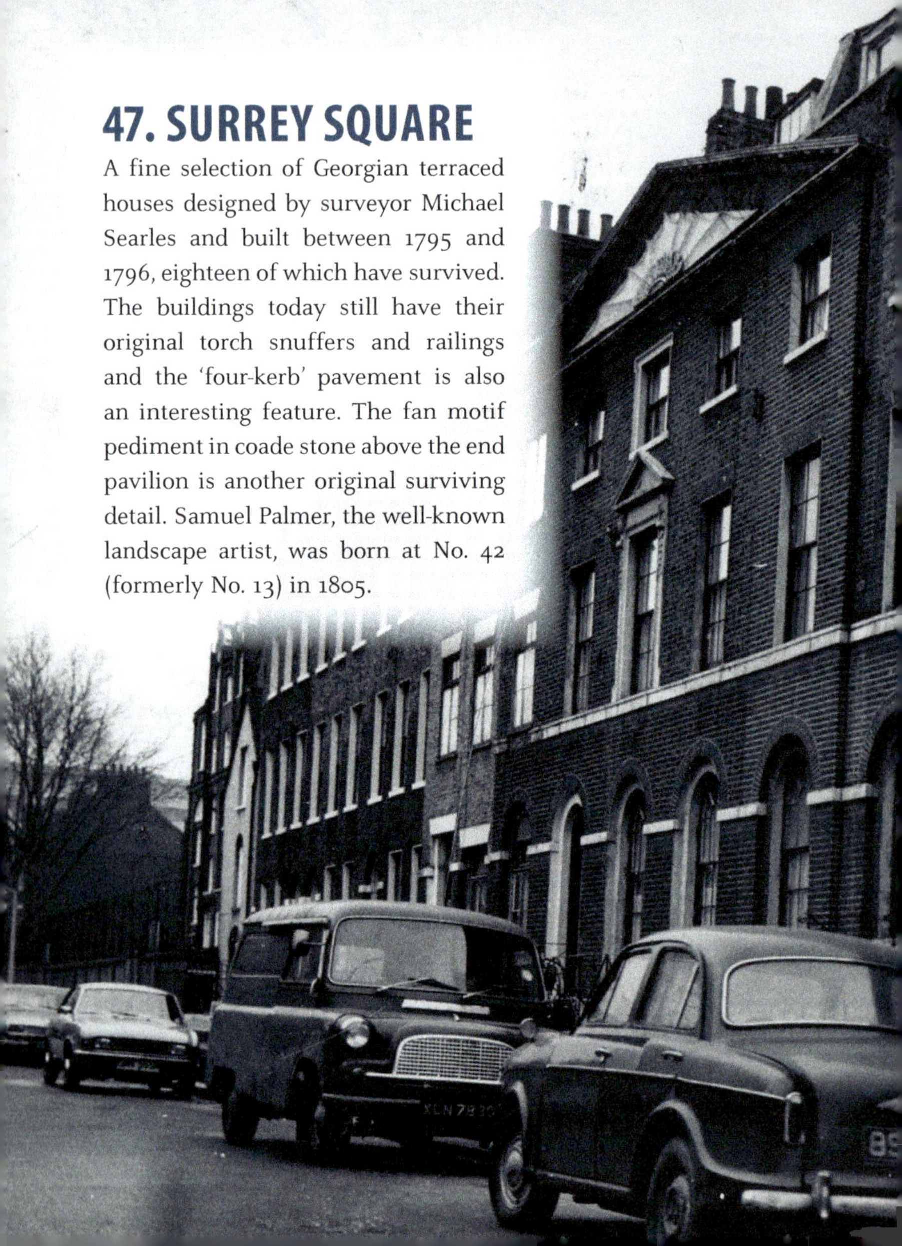

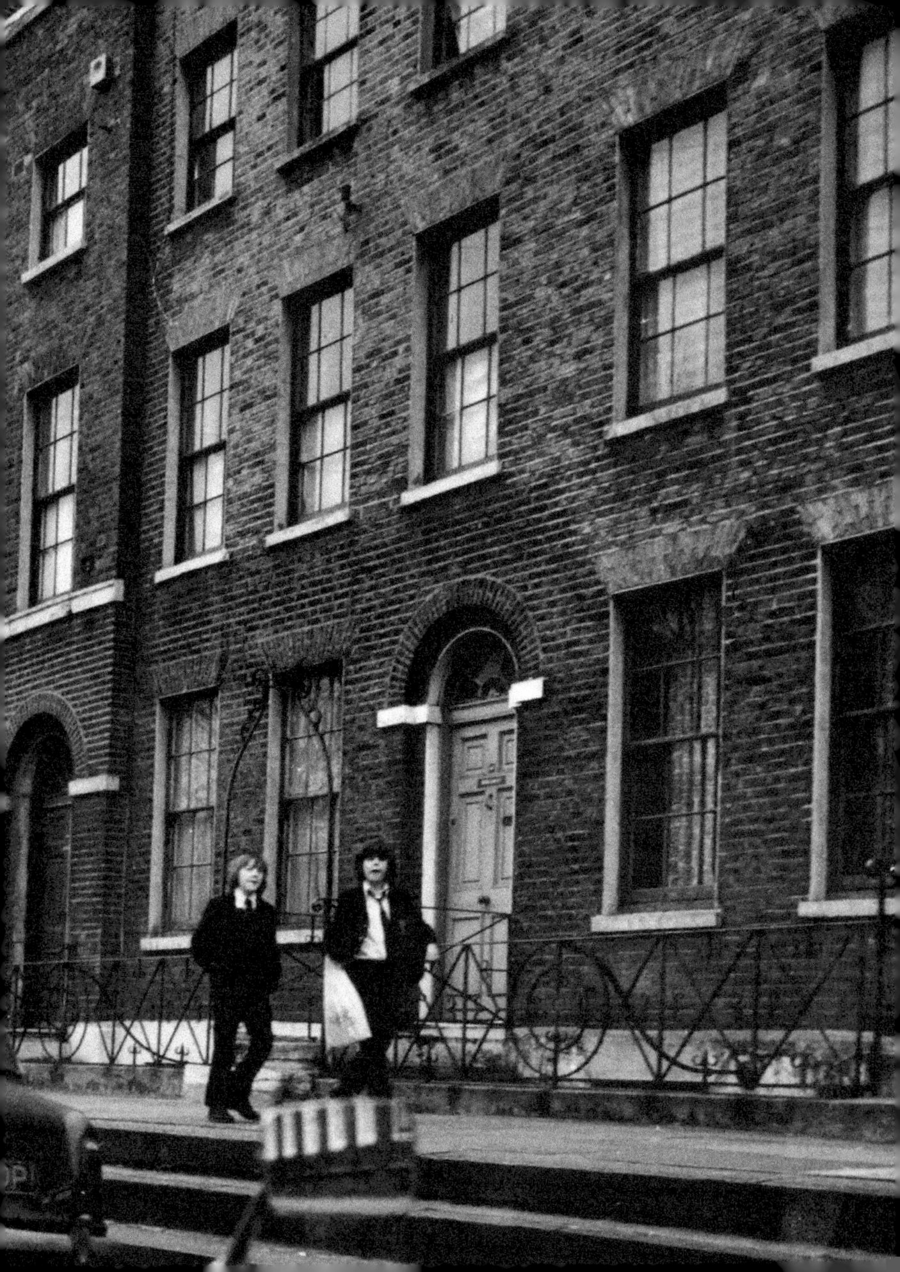

48. EXON STREET

Many of the houses in this quiet backwater near to the Old Kent Road have been saved and restored in recent years. The authors were particularly pleased to find the goal posts from the 1970s still there and ready for use.

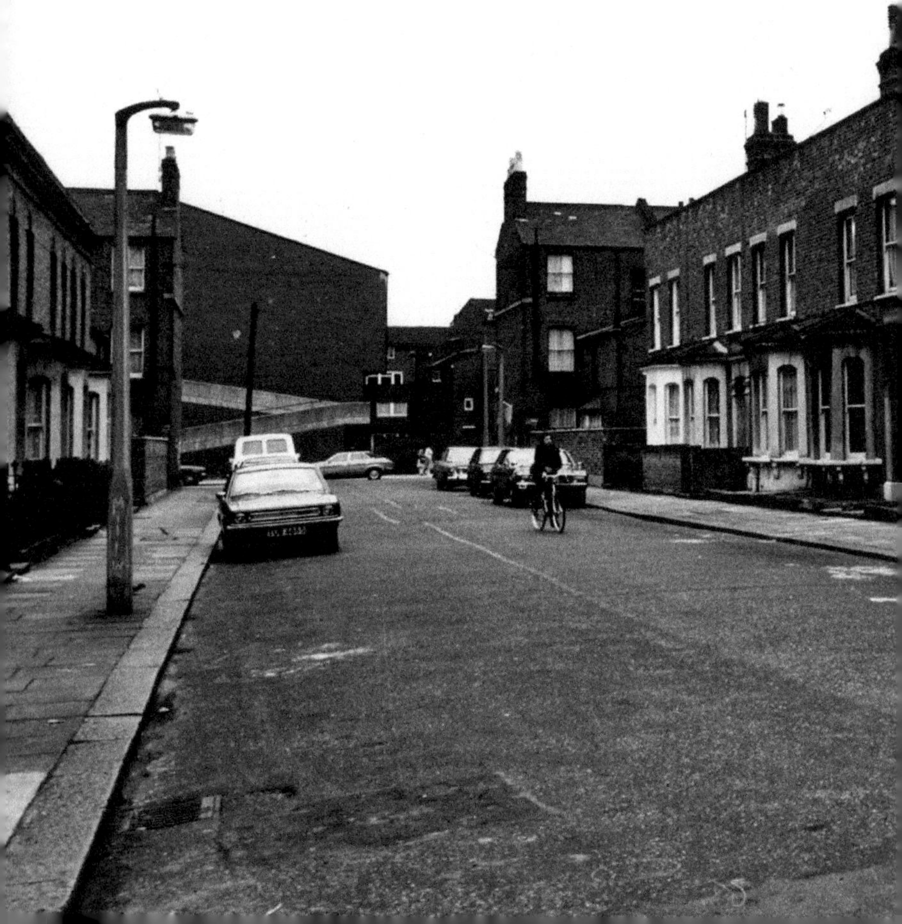

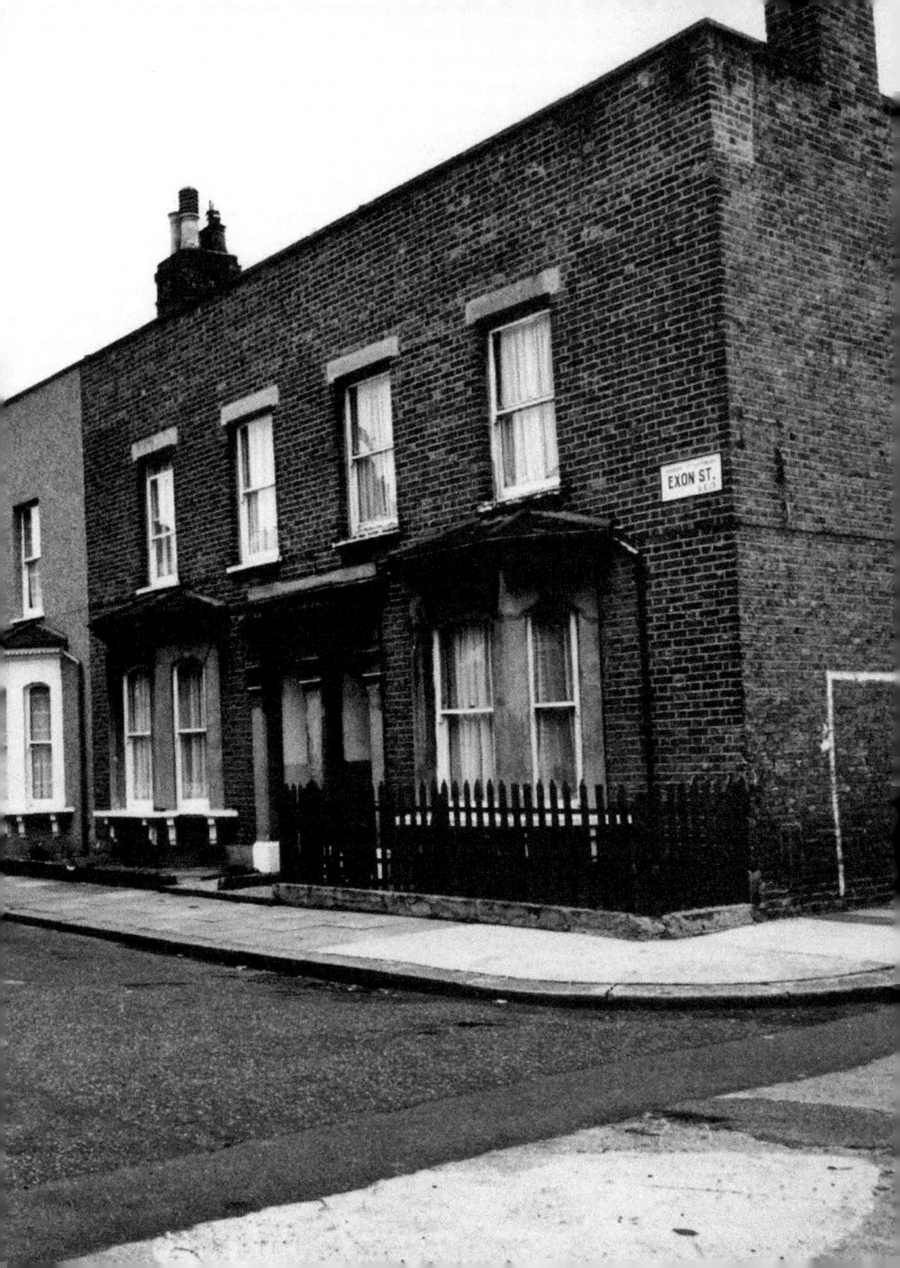
EXON ST.

49. THE HUNTSMAN & HOUNDS

Found on a quiet turning near to the East Street market, this fine looking pub has stood here at number 70 Elsted Street, on the corner of Tisdall Place since 1892. Many costermongers had their wedding receptions here in the 1920s and 1930s.

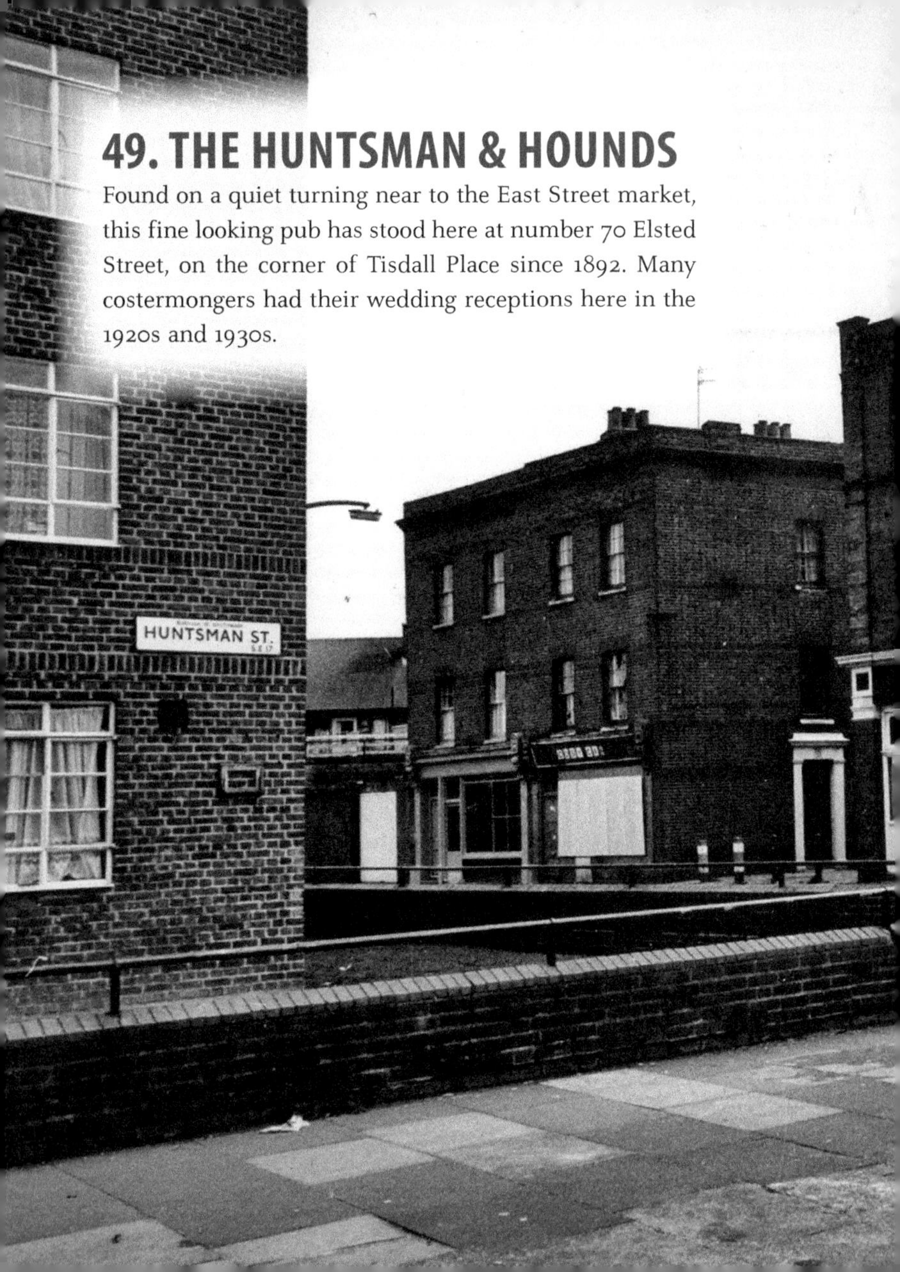

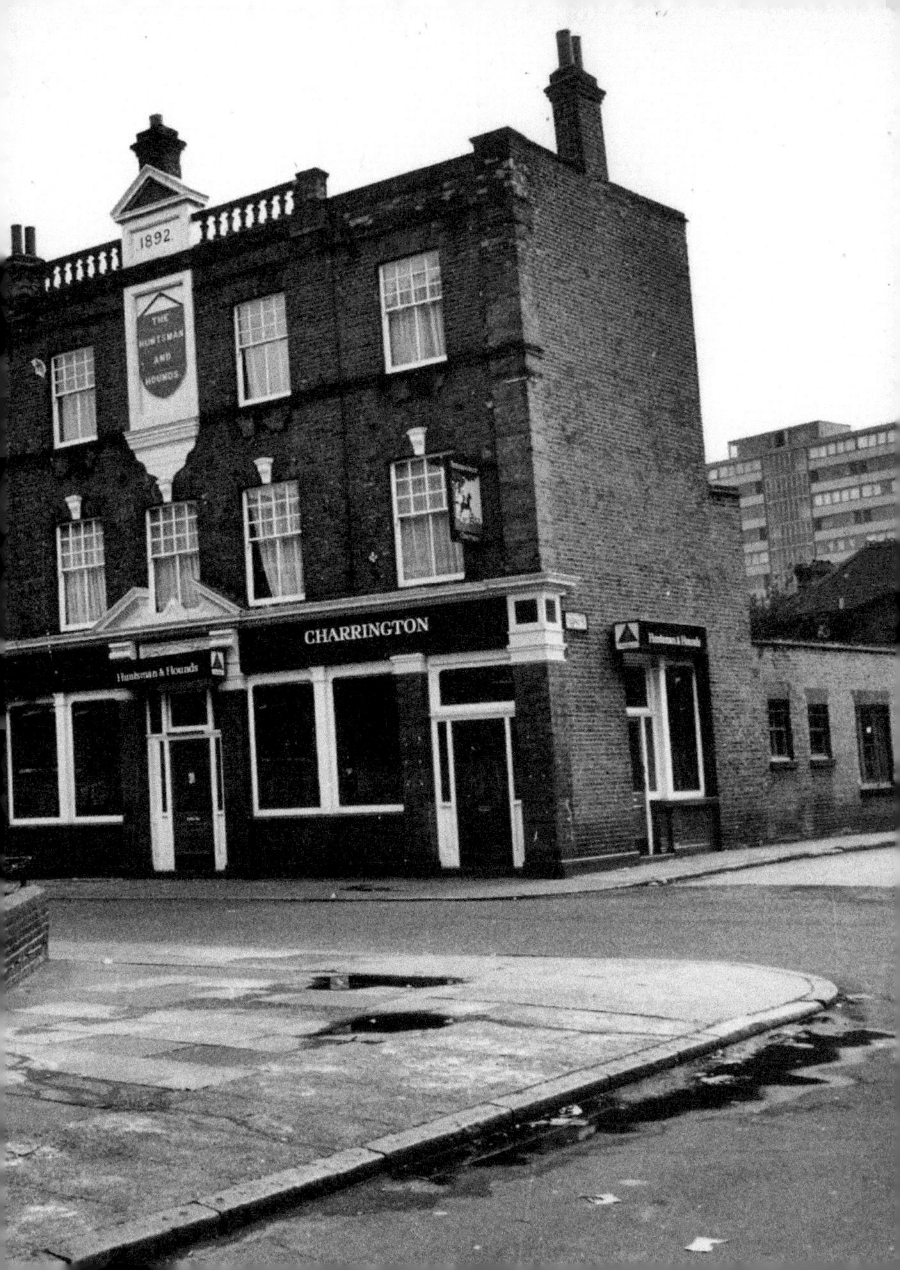
1892
THE HUNTSMAN AND HOUNDS
CHARRINGTON
Huntsman & Hounds
Huntsman & Hounds

50. KNOCKHOLT COTTAGES

Elsted Street, to the east of the Walworth Road, is the location for these cottages built in 1854, when most of the surrounding area would have been fields. Sometime in the last forty years they have lost the stone-carved pediment that proclaimed their name and the year they were built. A door and a window have also been lost and filled in with bricks and the original sash windows have been replaced.

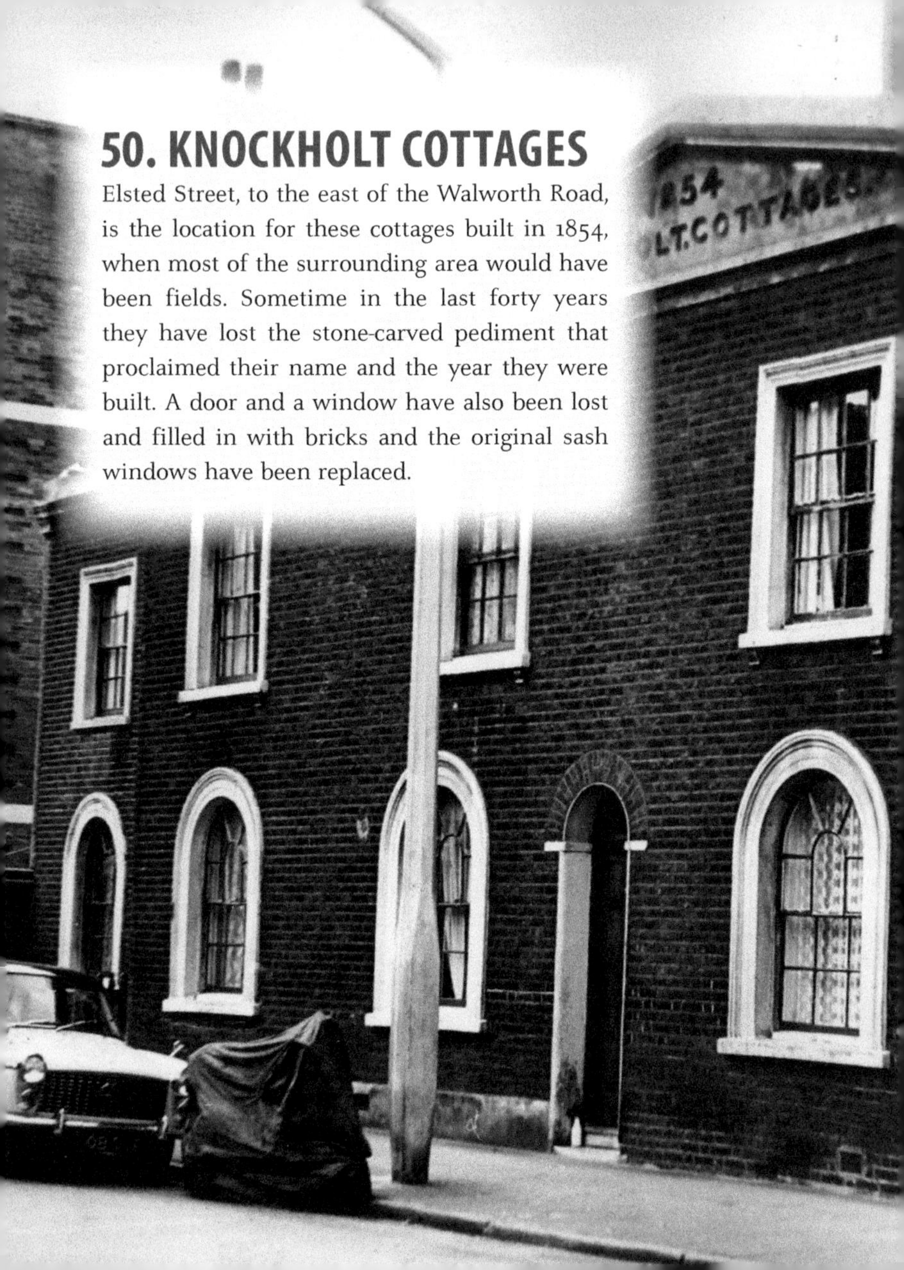